To Jon

The House With The Light On

A native Calgarian returns to the forties and fifties —
days of unlocked doors and carefree adventure

Eleanor King Byers

*Hope you find some
shared memories —
Enjoy!
Eleanor Byers*

Published in 2003 by Eleanor King Byers
1531 Varsity Estates Drive N.W.,
Calgary, Alberta, Canada T3B 3Y5

National Library of Canada Cataloguing in Publication Data
King Byers, Eleanor, 1937–
The house with the light on : a native Calgarian returns to the forties and fifties : days of unlocked doors and carefree adventure / Eleanor King Byers.

Includes bibliographical references.

ISBN 0-9733420-0-5

1. King Byers, Eleanor, 1937—Anecdotes.
2. Calgary (Alta.) —History—Anecdotes. I. Title.
FC3697.26.K56A3 2003   971.23'3802'092   C2003-911108-3

Layout/Design: Sherry Ward Design
Printing: Sundog Printing

Printed and bound in Canada

– DEDICATION –

To my brothers:

Stan, who delivered his lines as they were written
and
Don, who didn't

In loving memory of our parents:

Ruby Loan Hall Anderson
and
Horace King

who launched us with an inspiring script

. . . and kept the light on

– FOREWORD –

Ruben F. W. Nelson

Eleanor King Byers has captured what it was like to grow up in Calgary in the 1930s, '40s and '50s. With insight, good humour and a light touch, she brings to life the city and the times that shaped her and her generation. Through her eyes we see how children spent their time, where and how they played, and how they experienced the milkman and his horse, the Stampeders' first Grey Cup win, oiled roads and so much more.

If you lived in Calgary then, you will love this book. Eleanor has captured some of your life. The flood of memories will be reward enough. If you are new to Calgary or somewhat younger, you will enjoy her guided tour of what will often feel like another world.

The Calgary Eleanor reveals is very different from Calgary in 2003. Relationships then were both more important and more formal. The pace was gentler, seldom hurried. Play was more imaginative. Toys were fewer. Streets were safer. Children went out on Halloween together, but without their parents. And, their parents did NOT worry. Children knew most of their neighbours and their parents' friends by name. The consciousness that "time is money" did not dominate every waking moment. Medical care was more personal, but less effective. In sum, life felt both more spacious and more at the mercy of God.

How do I know? I was there. The "Mary" in some of the pictures is my sister. I knew Eleanor as one of my sister's gang. Eleanor's "Aunt Lil" was my mother's best friend. "Cousin Ritchie" and I were together in school, church, and the 18th Scout Troop.

We are all early '50s graduates of Sunalta Jr. High. I was then known as "Werthy" or "Butch" ...names that are still used by old friends.

I am thankful for this book for many reasons. It is an easy and delightful read. The tone is honest, not judgmental, and never overly sentimental. Eleanor is often self-revealing. You will like her. This is a non-trivial introduction to another time. People, places, events, attitudes and convictions are woven together in a way that captures the fabric of the times. Grandchildren may even come to see their grandparents in a new light! The "Updates" at the end of most chapters tell us the more recent fate of the key buildings and places.

Finally, as one who is passionate about both Calgary and our future, I am thankful for this book. Eleanor's stories make it clear that ours is a time of profound societal change. Calgary in the early 21st Century is not what it used to be. By 2055, Calgary will be quite different from today. As a futurist, I have found that exploring and understanding who we were and where we've come from can prepare us to meet the challenges of a changing future. My deepest desire is that we create our 21st Century Calgary with forethought, wisdom, courage and faith.

Ruben Nelson
Lac Des Arcs, Alberta
July 4, 2003

– SETTING THE STAGE –

Cast of Characters

Past:

Having never known any of my grandparents, I tend to think of them as Maria (as in "they call the wind . . .") & Reuben Anderson and Florence & Henry King. Reuben was "Grandpa" to my brothers for a few brief years, however, so with their references to "Grandpa" ringing in my ears, he occasionally creeps in as such.

My parents start out as Ruby Anderson and Horace King, because that's who they were—until they qualified as Mother and Dad. I don't think I was rigid about addressing my mother as "Mother," but I've always referred to her with this formality, because she liked formalities. That's not to say she wasn't fun.

I had three sets of aunts & uncles: Mildred & Walter King (Dad's brother), Millie & 'D' Snowden (Dad's sister), and Lil & Harry King (Mother's sister & Dad's brother). Don't let the latter confuse you. It's simple; sisters married brothers. And there's nothing incestuous—or illegal—about it.

Present:

My Walter King cousins are: Ethel, Art and Frank—names that have stood the test of time.

My Harry King 'double' cousins are: Marion, who we call Mar (as in 24 carat); Ritchie, who grew up to be Rich ☺; and Audrey, known to the family as Aud (as in odd), except she isn't. Honest.

Present *(continued...)*

My brother Stan has always been Stan, but Don was Donnie until he outgrew the last three letters.

Lastly, Me—Eleanor, Ellie or El depending on the circle I'm in. To my family I'm El, with the exception of my mother who always called me Eleanor—another reason for me to stick with "Mother." When my face pops up in the following pages, I'm Me.

The following recounting of past events has been written with every attention to detail—within the limitations of my memory. I initiated this project banking on the assistance of my brothers, each of whom leapt to my immediate aid with the identical nugget of information—our first phone number. It was R1761—invaluable to my story.

All dialogues have been presented in keeping with essential truths, my imagination only taking liberties when the truth got fuzzy. When I talk to myself, I speak in Italics. It helps me remember who I'm talking to.

The stage is set . . . dim the lights . . .

– CONTENTS –

–INTRODUCTION–

Bundle in a Basket

"It was a dark and stormy night. Outside, the wind was drawing spooky shadows on the front window as it whistled eerily round and round the house, and up and down the chimney. But inside, it was perfectly still. It was very late, and everyone was sound asleep in bed—everyone except me that is. I was in the living room reading my favorite book—The Count of Monte Cristo—and suddenly, there was a sharp rap on the door. I nearly jumped out of my skin. "Who's calling at this hour? What if it's a bogeyman!" My heart was going thump, thump, thump as I eased open the door—just a crack—then all of a sudden, a huge gust of wind blew it right out of my hand and crashed it against the wall. I thought for sure a bogeyman was going to jump out at me. But there wasn't any bogeyman. There wasn't anyone at all. I looked all around and finally stepped outside, just to make sure. That's when I heard it—a faint cry coming from below. I looked down, and there at my feet was a basket. Was I seeing things? The basket was moving! I crouched down for a closer look, and lo and behold, inside the basket was a tiny pink bundle wriggling for all it was worth. It seemed to be crying, "Here I am! Look in here!" Pinned to the bundle was a note. I had to get right down on my knees and lean in close to make out its words: "Please, **please** bring me inside and keep me warm."

...and that's what I did!"

"Daddy," I squeal, squirming with excitement in his lap, "that story's not really what happened, is it? That's not the way you got me. Tell me the *real* story."

Dad, an incurable storyteller with a boundless imagination, wraps me in his arms and insists, albeit hesitantly, "Of course that's how we got you. Right out of a wicker basket!"

"Daddy, tell the truth."

"Hmm—well—I'll tell you the *real* story on your tenth birthday."

Dad and I replayed this scene time and again throughout my childhood, the drama mushrooming with each intoxicating performance. I was hooked on the enchanting idea of being scooped from a stoop—especially since I was pretty sure I hadn't been. Now and then, however, Dad told the story with such conviction, I'd sneak off to Mother behind his back to solicit her variation on the theme—just for assurance. Mother's version wasn't nearly as gripping as Dad's, but for sure it was more believable, and better yet, she didn't make me wait until I was ten years old.

I was delivered by Dr. Alexander Fisher in the Holy Cross Hospital in the dead of night on Wednesday, September 22, 1937—a balmy, Indian summer night. Mother's recollection of the event was forever vague, claiming she'd been mercifully medicated into a twilight zone which offered her blessed release from the pain. As she gradually emerged from the fog cradling her newborn—the daughter she'd prayed for—the joy of her answered prayer was fleeting, lamentably nudged aside by the returning memory of her father's slow march toward death beyond her control.

My only surviving grandparent, now in the terminal stages of colon cancer, had been a welcome and cherished member of the household throughout my parents' marriage. Just weeks prior to my birth, Mother and Dad had tearfully placed Grandpa Anderson in the care of a nearby nursing home. I can't imagine the emotional roller coaster Mother rode that year, preparing her world for a new life as another slipped from her grasp.

Dad allowed himself only a brief inspection of his new daughter through the nursery window and a jubilant hug for his wife, before running the good news—quite literally—from Mother's bedside to the bedside of her father some blocks away. He could scarcely contain his excitement as he tiptoed down the dimly lit corridor of the nursing home, resolving to rouse Grandpa regardless of the hour or the objections of the nurses. Easing open the door to his room, he gasped at the sight of Grandpa, fully awake and sitting upright as if awaiting his arrival. Then with dancing eyes and a Cheshire cat grin, it was Grandpa who made the announcement, "It's a girl!" Dad initially reeled at the impossibility of this revelation, but quickly settled on the only possible explanation—an angel had delivered the news. It was a conjecture he embraced forever after. Grandpa Anderson died eight days later, and I would never touch his face, or feel his breath on mine. Mother would be denied a final farewell, her strict bed rest orders even forbidding her attendance at his funeral. I'm quite certain, however, that Grandpa's angel delivered a good-bye kiss from the two of us.

I know for sure, whether I'd burst through the door in a basket, or floated in on the wings of an angel, I'd struck gold. This family I'd landed was pure gold—a family that indeed answered the plea pinned to that tiny pink bundle. And so, with my family's warmth pinned to my memories, I embark on the journey we traveled together.

Two Warm Fuzzies

Preparations for my arrival were in full swing, orchestrated by the family's devoted nanny. Teresa had laundered nighties, nappies and blankets weeks before, but at the final hour, she rolled them through the steaming tubs one more time for good measure, hanging them on the line to absorb the sterilizing rays of the sun.

"When's our baby coming home, anyway?" eight-year-old Stan whines impatiently.

"Ya, when's she coming?" echoes four-year-old Donnie. "We've been waiting and waiting."

The question is repeated endlessly as the boys shadow Teresa throughout the day, all three unable to contain their excitement.

"Soon," Teresa assures them, attempting to hide her own impatience. "Mommy will bring your new sister home, soon."

"Those clothes are sure tiny," Donnie observes, as Teresa meticulously folds each fresh-as-all-outdoors item before tenderly tucking it into its designated drawer. "Our sister isn't that small, is she?"

The boys are so absorbed with questioning Teresa as she scurries about, they fail to hear Mother enter the nursery. She finds them poking their noses through the railings of my crib, watching in wide-eyed wonder as Teresa performs a final task they can't believe; she is reaching right down into the crib with a hot iron, to give the bedding a perfectly timed warming—a prophetic act considering Dad's "bundle in the basket" story has not yet entered his imagination.

My second warm fuzzy came from further afield, lovingly wrapped in pink paper, bound with miles of bright ribbon. Four years prior to my birth, a Christian movement called The Oxford

Group traveled across Canada, spearheaded by a spirited young woman named Eleanor Forde. Mother and Dad encountered the group at a rally in Banff and were immediately drawn to the ideology as well as its spokeswoman. Eleanor moved on, taking up permanent residence in the United States, but my parents' fleeting encounter with her was so profound, they christened me with her name. On receiving the flattering news, Eleanor promptly sent a gift to her namesake—a teddy bear, who was an instant favorite, and ultimately, a lifelong companion. Teddy's arms are mere stubs now, his button eyes are missing and he's entirely fuzzless, but the little guy is loved as much today as the day he arrived.

My parents adhered to the Oxford Group—later named Moral Re-Armament—for the rest of their lives, Dad assuming a leadership role for many years. But they lost touch with Eleanor Forde, and I never met her during these years. Yet Teddy and I always felt assured that she loved us, and subconsciously, we assigned her the role of our fairy godmother.

Then one day, years after my parents were gone, fortune delivered an inconceivable surprise. Conversation with a friend visiting from England revealed she knew Eleanor—now known as Ellie Forde Newton—and she supplied me with her Florida address. I wrote Ellie the very next day. A warm, enthusiastic response arrived by return mail, and a long distance friendship was born.

In April, 1999—six years after our first correspondence, and more than sixty years after Teddy first nestled in my crib—we met. My husband, Dick, and I, homebound from a South Africa trip via Miami, delayed the final leg of our journey to include a drive to Fort Myers Beach and the home of Ellie and her husband, Jim. They welcomed us with open arms and an indescribable spirit of generosity. We sat around their table sipping tea and chatting as though we were lifelong, intimate friends—as though Ellie and I just belonged together. A beloved friend accompanied us that day, because . . . well, because he insisted on coming along. Our hosts were utterly taken with him, and quickly awarded him star billing in our cozy circle. Teddy was the center of attention for the entire tea party.

Ellie Forde Newton with her 100th birthday Teddy from Me.
Husband Jim with my "namesake" Teddy from Ellie. 1999

I couldn't help noticing the enormous Canadian flag Ellie had draped over their porch in a patriotic demonstration of her undying love for her "home and native land." She described our day as golden and who could describe it better. Dick, overwhelmed by this amazing couple, took Ellie's hands in his as we reluctantly parted company, and blinking back the tears, declared, "Ellie, we've just been to South Africa and back on the trip of a lifetime, but today is the highlight of that trip." One month later Ellie celebrated her 100th birthday. Jim, six years her junior, died eight months after our visit at the age of ninety-four. In July 2003—the very week this book was finalized for press—Ellie died at the age of 104 years.

The Lord Giveth and The Lord Taketh Away

My eldest brother, Stan, was born on Tuesday, September 3, 1929 at Western Hospital, a small, intimate hospital located on Fourteenth Avenue West, just blocks from the family's residence. He was delivered by the next-door neighbor, Dr. Charles Bouck. Mother and Dad were ecstatic with their firstborn, and Grandpa Anderson was over the moon with his first grandchild. Then just one month later, on October 29—a date recorded in infamy—their idyllic world plummeted, along with that of the entire population. The stock market crash and the unimaginable consequences of the Great Depression to follow changed lives forever. The timing was especially bad for Dad's fledgling restaurant, a dispensable business that was surely doomed. Dad was noted for his positive attitude, even in the face of hopelessness, but with four mouths to feed in the middle of a depression, attitude wasn't enough. He had to come up with a practical solution, and quickly.

Gathering Stan in his arms one night, he somberly approached Mother with his answer to their financial crisis. "We must sell," he announced resolutely, "either the car or the baby." And that was the demise of the sleek, black, 1929 Nash with the gleaming spoked tires. I've not actually counted, but I'd swear our old box of photos holds more pictures of the car—and the dandy in knickers and diamond knee socks posing before it—than the baby, but it's a statistic I'd never be insensitive enough to point out to Stan. At least it was *him* they kept. Interestingly, the depression baby developed into a kid who demanded little more than the world had greeted him with. Stan could find a day's contentment with a cardboard box or two tin cans and a roll of wire.

Stan is now a retired medical doctor, living in Ottawa. We all envy the calm, contented disposition he's maintained since childhood. As the story goes, however, there was one momentous day he loudly and vigorously voiced his displeasure.

Dad & Mother on the right. A baby on the way; a dream car on the way out. 1929

Some Surprise

Don, the middle child, arrived on Wednesday, April 4, 1934, delivered by Dr. Albert Aikenhead, also at Western Hospital. Pregnancy was a hush hush subject back then, so big brother Stan was carefully protected from the facts of life, or any clear revelation of just what was about to intrude on his world. He only knew that, "Mommy has to go away for a while, but she'll bring you back a big surprise." Surprise? His imagination took flight, soaring for days over a multitude of inviting possibilities, finally landing on two by the time Mother gave him a departing kiss. For two weeks he tossed around the only two surprises he'd entertain, certain he'd get one, but secretly hoping for both.

When at last Mother returned, tenderly embracing the surprise as promised, he nearly knocked her down in the rush to see what it was. Breathlessly peeling back its wrapping, his eyes widened like saucers, then melted into a frown of disgust as he moaned, "Aw gee, I wanted a polar bear or a porcupine." And so, Don's grand entrance to center stage was panned by his big brother on opening night. When he developed into a kid frequently known to growl with discontent and prickle with impatience, we often reminded Stan, that in fact, his wish was granted.

Stan and his porcupine. 1935

Don went on to earn a Master's Degree in Fine Arts, and currently lives in Los Angeles. He's had a varied career as a stage manager and writer, but never again received a pan quite that blunt.

Update:

The Holy Cross Hospital closed its doors in March, 1996. It continues to serve the community's health through physician's offices, surgical suites and other related services.

Our beloved nanny, Teresa, moved to Seattle a few years after my birth, married and raised a family of four. We never saw her again, but Mother and I maintained a correspondence with her until her death in 1992.

Western Hospital on Fourteenth Avenue Southwest, between Second and Fourth Streets, closed in 1947. Apartments are now situated on the site.

The Anderson Family; Reuben, Lillian, Ruby, Maria. circa. 1916

Chapter 1

—BEGINNINGS—

Sophisticated Sisters

Mother was born December 1, 1902, in Montreal, Quebec, the eldest of two daughters born to Reuben and Maria Anderson. Reuben, forty-two years old when his firstborn arrived, had long nurtured a dream of a son and namesake, but willingly settled for Ruby in place of Reuben. If there was a trace of disappointment with her gender or that of her sister Lillian to follow, it was well concealed. The sun rose and set on the two curly haired moppets.

Not long after the birth of Lillian in 1906, Reuben developed tuberculosis, and the ensuing events altered their lives forever. The recommended treatment for Reuben was rest and a change of climate to Alberta's sunny skies and clean, dry air, where outdoor work was prescribed to maximize the benefits. Reuben begrudgingly resigned the job he loved as a telegrapher for the Montreal Star and ventured west to scout for an outdoor job and a home for his young family. He arrived in Calgary in May of 1907, and the family followed in late October.

Not until the Calgary Street Railway was launched in 1909 did Reuben find the ideal outdoor job, as a conductor, but the first summer he did fulfill his doctor's "outdoor" orders to the letter, by sleeping in a tent in the back yard. He recovered fully and maintained good health for the next thirty years.

Maria, a skilled seamstress, took in sewing as well as an

occasional boarder to supplement the family income. But she never adjusted to the disheartening separation from her Eastern family, especially her beloved sister Sadie, who was married to Reuben's brother Clayton, and I now sense her eternal longing must have spilled into her eldest daughter's psyche. There always seemed to be a void in my mother's life, that I could never quite put a finger on.

A rare visit from the Eastern Family; Reuben, Cousin Marj, Maria, Aunt Sadie, Ruby, Lillian, Mr. Dickens (the boarder). circa.1914

The Andersons were poor by anyone's standards, but Maria concealed the fact with her regal manner and her ability to produce elaborate wardrobes for herself and her daughters, sometimes even piecing together little dresses out of fabric salvaged from Reuben's discarded suits. The girls, always groomed to perfection, were raised with the impeccable manners of a finishing school and a solemn respect for their elders, much to the appreciation of the surrounding neighbors.

The Andersons can be traced to four different Calgary addresses, but only one—216 - 4th Avenue West—seemed to hold any significance for Mother, and a nostalgic drive past her favorite house when we were kids, would launch an oft repeated tale from inside its walls. The Prince residence—now a familiar attraction in Heritage Park—stood on the corner of their block, and the Smith sisters lived next door, with their aloof gentleman boarder, who was apparently too burdened with weighty matters to pay them any heed. I'm quite sure Maria would have coached her little darlings to curtsy whenever the boarder passed by, had she foreseen his destiny as their Prime Minister. In any event, she looked on with pride the day the girls stilled their skipping ropes at the sight of Mr. R. B. Bennett approaching, and without their mother's prompting, stood reverently aside as he strode past without awarding them so much as a nod or a smile.

The girls had a more rewarding encounter with Mr. Bennett at a later date, however, when they donated a bouquet of flowers to an auction in aid of the war effort. They attached a note, painstakingly written in their combined hands, reading, "We are two little girls named Ruby and Lillian, who would like to help our King." To their delight, Mr. Bennett purchased their flowers, and the next day, a hand delivered note arrived at their door expressing his gratitude, "I bought your bouquet. Thank you. May you live long to help your King." They did.

Two men rose to the top of their favorite list—Mr. Nanthrup, proprietor of the confectionery down the alley, and George, the beloved street cleaner. The girls got to go to Mr. Nanthrup's for ice cream cones on the rare occasion when there was a nickel left over after their weekly deposit at Sunday School. Mr. Nanthrup had an ingeniously designed scoop with a deep 'V' extending from the rounded part, so that when he scooped the ice cream it took on the shape of the entire cone. Getting the ice cream *into* the cone, however, was tricky. He'd have to invert it onto wax paper, place the cone over the now exposed pyramid, and flip the whole thing upright. Needless to say, Mr. Nanthrup's securely anchored ice cream never tumbled off their cones.

George was a kindly, bearded, black man who wore overalls and kept their streets clean, summer and winter. It's little wonder that George stood so tall in the minds of two little girls who were raised with the edict that cleanliness is next to godliness. In a letter to me, written in her nineties, Aunt Lil relayed a number of tales regarding George, highlighted with her favorite about the day she lost her glasses in the snow—catastrophic for a child as short sighted as she—and George found them with his shovel. Having observed where the little girl with the glasses lived, he delivered them safely to the front door. "I now know he kept a protective eye on us, as well as keeping our street clean," she said. "Uncle George was our guardian angel. I hope he got his wings."

Braemar Lodge, a legendary residential hotel with mostly upper class, mature, single residents, was located directly across the street, and although the girls were constantly admonished not to stare, the straight-laced Maria had trouble resisting the temptation herself. I can see her standing motionless in the center of the parlor, peering through the lace curtains to watch, undetected, the intriguing women rocking on the front porch. They were unlike any women Maria knew in her world confined to school, church and home. (From all descriptions, Maria made it her mission to shelter her daughters from the ominous world outside these same three boundaries.)

"Look at that sinful woman with the painted face," Maria gasps, as one more wanton woman in full makeup joins the Braemar porch circle. "She's puffing on a cigarette, too. Doesn't that beat all. Tch! Tch!"

But her mutterings are largely ignored, because the girls are entirely preoccupied with the stately passerby, Mrs. A. A. Dick, who their mother had, on a previous occasion, identified as a survivor of the luxury liner, *Titanic*.

"Do you think she's a ghost?" Lillian asks her knowledgeable big sister. Ruby intuitively knows that, to her little sister, it's a perfectly reasonable question, and she would not think of ridiculing her.

"Oh no, Lillian," she replies solemnly, "she's a real live person."

"But didn't everyone drown?" persists Lillian.

"No, lots of people were rescued in lifeboats. Mrs. Dick was one of the lucky ones."

Lillian had sweet dreams that night, understanding for the first time that the entire passenger list did not go down with the *Titanic*.

The Anderson's entertainment budget was meager, so it was a rare occasion when Reuben spirited the girls off to the Pantages Theater, in spite of Maria's disapproval, which always made the girls feel guilty for enjoying it so much. The family took only one real holiday together—a whole week at the Homestead Hotel in Banff, where Mother learned to swim at the Cave and Basin. She talked about it to her dying day.

Cave and Basin Beauties. Lillian, Ruby. circa. 1914

Mother loyally attended Central Methodist Church, twice every Sunday, then returned mid week for a much loved evening with her CGIT group. She received her education at the *Old Central School*, Central Collegiate Institute and finally, Normal School, newly located at the Provincial Institute of Technology and Art, where she obtained her Teacher's Certificate.

Normal School was delayed for a time, however, when Mother accepted the formidable responsibility of full time caregiver for her dying mother. It would be a complete role reversal for this young, sheltered woman, whose own needs had, until then, been the sole focus of her mother. Maria eventually retreated to the darkened recesses of the home, to hide from the shocking disfigurement of a malignancy cruelly gnawing away at her beautiful face. It broke Mother's heart. She was just twenty-two when Maria drew her last breath, her frightened, inconsolable nursemaid clutching her hand.

Boisterous Brothers

My father was born in Preston, Lancashire, England on February 17, 1902, the youngest of Henry and Florence King's seven children, the first two children having died in infancy. Driven by their sense of adventure, the surviving family set sail from Liverpool for the 'Land of Promise' on the *S. S. Canada* on June 15, 1905—four boisterous brothers and their lone, adored sister in the middle of the pack—Arthur, Walter, Mildred (known as Millie), Henry (known as Harry) and Horace, my father. My grandfather, Henry, was a qualified watchmaker, as well as an accomplished vocalist. His booming bass voice occasionally rang forth in light opera, and regularly in the Methodist Church choir. Under his arm, Henry carried the sign from his jewelry store window, advertising, "H. C. King's Lucky Wedding Rings," and in his heart, a passion for music, as he led his tribe first to Grenfell, Saskatchewan for five years, then on to Wainwright, Alberta for the next five.

The King Family; Henry, Arthur, Florence, Millie,
Horace (in Florence's desperation vice grip), Harry, Walter. 1905

Henry established jewelry businesses in each location, but there was no concealing the fact that his first love was music. He devoted many hours to training young voices, conducting choirs and producing a steady stream of concerts. The Elite Theatre in Wainwright fairly hopped with H. C. King's *Thanksgiving Great Patriotic Banquet, Concert and Dance,* not to mention his Easter Monday extravaganza—*Maid Marion & Robin Hood, an Operetta in VI Acts*—boasting "Sixty Performers and Magnificent Costumes." It also promised "Quaint Music, Melodies and Mirth," and you can rest assured it delivered. As one might expect, Henry and his offspring received star billing in each concert, as preserved playbills attest. My father, the baby of the family, no doubt reached his pinnacle with his lead role in *Dick Whittington And His Cat*. He played the cat. Florence slaved behind the scenes making the "magnificent costumes," but never received a credit on the playbills.

Florence's
"Magnificent Costumes"

Henry; unidentifed role.
England, circa. 1900

Millie; songstress. circa. 1915

Harry as Robin Hood. 1915

Descriptions of the family's standard of living suggest it was sparse, which wasn't surprising since the head of the house preferred conducting concerts over minding a jewelry store. Yet Dad was always quick to emphasize they never went hungry, even though the dinner menu was occasionally reduced to a single item—boiled potatoes.

Dad had a favorite story of the Wainwright Hotel—a hotel familiar to present day Calgarians in its reconstructed form in Heritage Park. As a young lad he passed the hotel every day on his way to and from school, and discovered its wooden porch provided a welcome distraction to the journey, if he skipped along it with his boots tapping in rhythm to the clickety clack of a stick he'd drag along the railing. When his mother got wind of his annoying habit—and the resulting complaints from disgruntled hotel guests—she forbade him to step foot on the porch again "under any circumstance." Fearing God might strike him dead if he disobeyed, he altered his route to bypass all temptation. One day a monstrous hailstorm hit town just as he was making his way home from school. The hotel porch was the obvious place to seek shelter—except that his mother's orders, "not under any circumstance" unquestionably denied him the option. And so, poor little Horace bravely battled his way home under a barrage of hailstones that pummeled him mercilessly throughout the entire trek. He arrived battered and bruised, but with one thing proudly intact—his honor.

Life might have coasted along in Wainwright indefinitely had the Great War not intervened, springing the patriotic Kings into action. Henry and the two eldest sons, Arthur and Walter, enlisted in the Canadian Army, and were posted overseas, Henry in the role of a bandmaster. Florence, feeling abandoned, scooped up the other three children and returned to Preston, where she opened her heart and her kitchen to homesick Canadian servicemen. It's interesting to note that during the family's ten years in Canada, they'd become steadfast Canadians. They discarded their British accents, proudly served in the Canadian Army and, even in their homeland, referred to themselves as Canadians.

In the dying stages of the war, on April 19, 1918, the family received the news every family with a son on the battlefront dreads. Arthur, age twenty-three, their beloved eldest, had fallen victim to a sniper's bullet in France. The shattering loss exacted a terrible toll on the family, and utterly destroyed Florence. It took all their will to carry on, yet carry on they did and in 1919 they once again set sail for their adopted country, as planned.

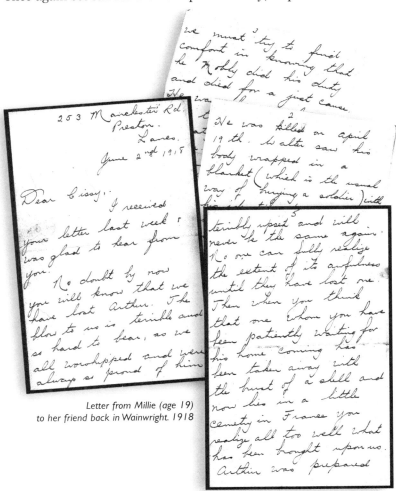

Letter from Millie (age 19)
to her friend back in Wainwright. 1918

Dad was a seventeen-year-old with a disrupted and incomplete education when his family arrived in Canada the second time, this time settling in Calgary. He was blessed with the inherent savvy of an entrepreneur, however, and effortlessly entered the jewelry business with his father, developing into a skilled watchmaker under his tutelage. But he knew from the beginning it was not for him, and restlessly kept an eye on the horizon for other possibilities.

Meanwhile, my grandmother was gathering confidence as an authority on antiques, having directed many hours to studying the subject during her wartime interval in England. An armload of reference books accompanied her back to Canada, and after months of burning the midnight oil with further study, the time had come: she plunked herself down at her desk, took a deep breath, and boldly drew up her first order.

The arrival of that first shipment from England transformed Florence overnight from a woman immobilized with despair to a woman on the move. Her dream of her own antique business had reached fruition and there was no stopping her. Henry, helplessly infected with his wife's enthusiasm, closed the door on his jewelry store and stepped into the antique business at her side. The four children also collaborated on the new enterprise, although Walter and Harry continued to maintain previously established teaching careers. And so, The Calgary Antique Store—later named The House of Antiques—was born, operating from the family's residential address at 220 - 7th Avenue West.

The antique shop was no sooner rolling, when fate tempted the family with another opportunity. Their demanding lives frequently necessitated a quick bite to eat at the Tea Kettle Inn restaurant, conveniently located just two doors east of their residential business. A warm friendship soon developed with Mrs. Watson, its elderly owner, and when the time came for her to retire, the Kings were the natural choice to step in. She approached them with the idea, and without hesitation, a deal was struck. The Kings were off and running again. Still banding together, as immigrants often do, all family members were involved in the decision-making of the second enterprise, but Millie and Horace were the most available to carry out the hands-on operation. From the moment Aunt Millie and Dad stepped through those doors, they knew this was their calling, and effortlessly slipped into a winning, lasting partnership. Little did the Kings know, that from these humble beginnings, would unfold two establishments that Calgarians would fondly embrace and long remember.

A Prince, A Princess and A King

My father,
Horace King
1923

My mother,
Ruby Anderson
1923

In the twenties, the singles crowd that Mother and Dad adhered to gathered at two places on the weekend: Penley's Dance Hall, where they danced to Mart Kenny's Orchestra, under a rigid dress and behavioral code; and the Prince's Island Tennis Courts, where a high level of decorum was also expected. I have difficulty visualizing my mother playing tennis, but I do know that her career on the courts lasted at least long enough to seal the love match of her life. Dad's version of their meeting had it taking place in the summer of 1920, when he arrived for a pick-up game, spotted the petite, dark-haired beauty on the court, and asked his friend—who was conveniently her next door neighbor—for an introduction to "the girl he planned to marry." After some years of diligent courting, always bearing two ice cream cones—one for her younger sister—he won her hand, and on July 19, 1927, a Tuesday, his bold prophecy came true at the Pro Cathedral Anglican Church in downtown Calgary.

Prince's Island Tennis Club; R.B. Bennett (center) Patron. circa. 1922

I have always lamented the absence of grandparents in my life, yet the void was amply filled by a matchless, though compact, extended family of three aunts, three uncles and six cousins. To our everlasting delight, Mother and her sister Lillian followed in the footsteps of their mother and her sister, by marrying brothers—Lillian married Harry—and to our ever, *ever*lasting delight, the two quiet, reserved Anderson sisters never succeeded in taming the loud, unruly King brothers, though God knows they tried. I suspect the lone sister of these rowdies, our Aunt Millie, and her lovable giant of a husband, Uncle 'D' (DeWitt Snowden), loved these jokesters just the way they were. On the other hand, Uncle Walter's sweet, gentle wife, our Aunt Mildred,* remains a question mark. A born diplomat, she would never reveal her sentiments, nor would she have attempted to change anyone, even if she thought they needed fixing. And so, the King brothers never got *fixed*, and whenever we all gathered under one roof, mayhem ensued—and we loved it!

*We referred to Walter's wife as "Mildred," while calling Dad's sister of the same name, "Millie."

Update:

Mother's childhood residence was nudged aside by the International Hotel.

Central Methodist Church's interior was heavily damaged by fire in 1916, but was restored and re-opened a year later. In 1925 it became Central United, Calgary's first United Church following the union of Methodists, Congregationalists and Presbyterians.

The *Old* Central School at Fifth Avenue and First Street West, later became James Short, and is now reduced to a lonely cupola on a parking lot.

Central Collegiate Institute, which Mother attended, was Central High School by the time I walked its hallowed, creaking halls.

SAIT's first building where Mother attended Normal School, is now known as Heritage Hall. Ironically, due to lack of funds, it escaped demolition, and underwent a two-year renovation, completed in 2001, restoring it to a near replication of its original majesty.

I was overjoyed to discover on a lobby wall in the Wainwright Hotel at Heritage Park, a framed invitation to an Easter Monday Concert under concertmaster H. C. King, urging one and all to come in "laughing trim." My research places the year as 1914. And Grandma, I do stroll the porch, but never dragging a stick along the railing.

I have visited my "unknown soldier," Uncle Arthur, both at the Canadian National War Memorial in Vimy, France, and at the War Memorial in the town of Wainwright, Alberta.

The frontage of the prized King family residence, which doubled as their business address — 220-7th Avenue West — is largely obscured by an LRT station, but my image of its eye-catching neon sign, in the form of a hanging tea kettle, remains crystal clear.

Penley's Dance Hall closed in 1964.

The Prince's Island Tennis Courts are gone, but Calgary's premiere, inner city park which housed them, is in full swing.

Chapter 2

—A CORNER IN CONNAUGHT—

Mother and Dad's first home was at 739 - 12th Avenue West, an unpretentious stucco bungalow standing on the southeast corner of Twelfth Avenue and Seventh Street Southwest. A tall, green, lattice fence enclosed the back yard, and a big caragana hedge rimmed the front. Still reeling from the aftershock of the depression at the time of my arrival, Dad's solution to feeding another mouth was to supplement the income by duplexing the house. And so, as the family grew, the little bungalow shrank. The main floor's bedroom wing was expropriated for the rental apartment, and our sleeping quarters were established in the basement. Even though Dad designed the project with separate entrances and back yards to maintain privacy for all, Mother never grew to like the arrangement, and steadfastly maintained forever after, that when the house was eventually sold, expenses had still not been recovered. Knowing her common sense approach to money and budgeting, I suspect she was right.

We lived at '739' until just prior to my sixth birthday, making memories of that location vague and isolated for me. Often I'm unsure whether an image is my own, or one I've conjured from listening to the family's repeated stories. I've therefore relied heavily on my brothers' memories for the construction of this portion of my tale.

The five of us at '739'. 1938

The War Years

Most of my Beltline years coincided with the war, so memories largely revolve around its day to day effect on us. Even though we were blessedly spared the direct ravages of war, its magnitude was surprising, influencing everything, from food and clothing supplies, to our very play activity.

I remember Mother receiving ration books containing coupons for scarce food items, such as meat, dairy products and sugar, color coded for each item. The ration books received the same fastidious attention as her bank book, so we never ran short, nor do I recall any real hardship. Mother's faithful adherence to the dietary dictates of our pediatrician, Dr. Harold Price, warning against pop, candy or sweets of any kind, actually produced a surplus of sugar coupons at the end of the month. As an aside, Dr. Price also advised against pickles, although I don't think any of us, including Mother, actually knew why. We only knew they never graced our table. I still don't eat them, but at least now I know why. I don't like them.

Mother progressed from a child of meager means to a bride of the depression, then ten years later to the constrictions of a world war. It's no wonder she was firmly programmed to never waste a morsel of food. How often did I hear her repeat, "Think of all the starving children in Greece," as I stared grimly at the forlorn carrots growing cold on my plate. She must have seen a particularly heart-rending newsreel about Greece, because it remained her starvation location throughout my entire childhood. Unfortunately, all the sympathy in the world for the children of Greece never improved the taste of carrots.

Plastic food containers and wraps were a thing of the future, and I can still see Mother frugally stashing the most minuscule amount of leftovers—like maybe 8 or 10 peas—into a teacup with the saucer for a lid, for storage in our pint-sized refrigerator, already chock full of teetering teacups. Some years later, we acquired a cat who existed on teacup scraps, and she was absolutely mad about peas. One day I carefully concealed my uneaten carrots in her dish of peas, ever so pleased with myself for solving my carrot dilemma once and for all. My heart sank as I watched her meticulously nose her way through her dish, eating every single pea and leaving behind every morsel of carrot. I knew then and there, Smoky was a very smart cat. When she got tired of teacup scraps, or they'd been dumped into a stew, she purred over a dish of bread soaked in warm milk. But she would have starved before eating a carrot.

For my brother Stan, eight years older than I, the war held great fascination and it often became the basis for his creative entertainment. Calgary was a prime air training center during the war, fighter pilots filling the skies with a steady buzz and every boy's imagination with dreams of heroism. Stan flew Harvards in his sleep. He was beside himself the day his mail order Orphan

Annie Flying Kit arrived, a realistic set of controls for a plane—made from sturdy cardboard—which he assembled and belted himself into for a day's flying—vr-r-o-m, vr-r-o-o-m, vr-r-o-o-m, in perfect formation with the Harvards above.

I have a clearer memory of Stan building a model Thunderbolt—a U.S. fighter plane—out of balsam and paper. The project seemed so delicate, I'd actually tiptoe into his room to watch him at work, almost afraid to speak for fear of disturbing something. Patiently, he cut each section with a fine knife, following the model's plans to the letter, and as he glued it together inch by inch, I thrilled at the sight of a slowly emerging plane. Then one day—I remember it being twilight—I pushed open the door to his bedroom, and in the dim stillness of the room, something floated eerily above my head. As my eyes adjusted to the light, I slowly realized what it was—the Thunderbolt! Now fully assembled, and hanging by a string from the ceiling, I had stirred it into silent motion. I resisted turning on the light and losing the mood, and instead, crept further into the room to sit on the edge of Stan's bed. There I remained, never taking my eyes off that Thunderbolt until it was still.

Stan's interest in planes extended to collecting the airplane cards found in Crackerjacks. Every week he blew his allowance on a five cent box of Crackerjacks, and although he liked the caramel coated popcorn, the cards were the main inducement to buy. The cards, on heavy card stock, with rounded corners and full descriptions on the back, presented allied fighters, bombers, or transports, mainly British and American, in realistic color. Stan traded and collected until he completed the full set of 150 cards. Well into our adulthood, the set resided in our grandfather's flip-down oak desk. Then one day they mysteriously took flight. We still have the desk, but I doubt the Antique Road Show would appraise it at half the value of the cards.

Stan had another collection that does survive today—a 100-page scrapbook entirely devoted to the 1939 Royal Visit of King George VI and Queen Elizabeth to Canada. Canadians were devoted monarchists, so the tour grabbed headlines everywhere it went, and the scrapbook was quickly filled to capacity. Calgarians turned out in droves when the revered couple arrived by train on May 26, toured the city by car, and then re-boarded the train for Banff. Their motorcade rolled down Thirteenth Avenue, one short block from our home, so the family raced south to the corner to wave hello, then raced the two blocks north to the railroad tracks to wave good-bye. No one left the tracks until the train had entirely disappeared from view.

My all-time favorite photo of my brothers and me was taken on that occasion, the three of us aboard one trike. Stan is sitting at the helm, holding a Canadian Red Ensign; Don is standing behind, on the lower step, with his flag tucked into his overalls; and I'm sandwiched in-between, on the upper step. I must have sensed the electricity in the air on that history making day, even though I was too young to grasp its significance.

Waiting for the King and Queen. 1939

Stan also inherited a Morse Code set of Grandpa's, and would tap out dots and dashes in his bedroom by the hour. I don't think he ever had the patience to learn the actual code, but carried off the tapping with such flair, who would have known. He set up a second communication device between our bedrooms—tin cans with paper diaphragms, connected by a stretched linen thread running through the adjoining heat registers. I loved this intriguing way of communicating with the ally, though I was never sure whether the voice was coming from the can or the heat register.

My favorite wartime event was the blackout, a defense drill where the entire city turned out the lights against possible air invasion by night. We were allowed the use of candles and flashlights, but only if the windows were adequately sealed. Blackouts offered the perfect set of circumstances for us kids; an opportunity to participate in the excitement of the war, by hiding on the enemy—an intangible enemy—in the pitch dark.

I made it a game to creep from window to window spying for planes, giving Mother a nervous breakdown every time I pulled a curtain back in violation of the exercise.

"Mother, who's that?" I asked one night, my heart racing at the sight of two ghostly silhouettes standing motionless in front of the confectionery across the street. They were the only sign of life on a street completely devoid of vehicles, pedestrians, house lights or street lamps. I was so spooked, I could hardly breathe. Then the figures moved, and Mother and I both recognized the outlines of Dad and Hymie Crystal, the proprietor of the store. Only then did it occur to me, that I'd never before seen these two men engaged in social exchange. It took a total city shutdown to free them from their demanding businesses for a friendly, whispered conversation in the dark.

Don's interests differed entirely from Stan's and mine. Don had little use for airplanes, communication gadgets, blackouts, or anything to do with the war. He also didn't care for children his own age, and in fact, was rather uncomfortable with contemporaries, much preferring the company of adults. He therefore spent those Beltline years parading the block, and calling on the neighborhood women, who freely welcomed little Prince Charming into their kitchens for peanut butter sandwiches and conversation.

Mrs. Allison and her car were a major attraction. Her fabulous Ford coupe was enticing itself, but a woman at the wheel transcended all. He used to watch for her returning from work, then dash down the alley and throw open her garage doors in readiness. His reward was to climb up into the front seat beside her, where he'd perch like a dandy for all to see, as they glided into the garage. Then he'd be off on his rounds for more food and gifts, fully aware of his ability to charm adults, expecting his due. Interestingly, our wise and watchful mother remained trustingly unconcerned about Don's extended absences, a freedom he cherishes even more today, when he observes the current generation of children, whom he claims are organized, supervised and monitored to death.

A Hunky-Dory Retreat

Gull Lake. 1940

Some of the happiest memories of our young lives took place plunk in the middle of the war—during magical summer holidays at *Hunky-Dory*, a rustic cabin at Gull Lake, Alberta, which our family shared with our cousins. *Hunky-Dory* came loaded with all the compelling features that our boring old city house lacked: a huge stone fireplace, coal oil lamps on the mantle that Mother carried from room to room like Florence Nightingale, walls that stopped short of the ceiling, a screened-in sleeping porch stretching clear across the front, a wood-burning stove in the kitchen, an ice box in the pantry, a water pump down the road, and best of all, an outhouse out back. All this, plus a veritable army of bats and mice, produced our own Magic Kingdom.

Me, Dad, Don. 1939

Our *Hunky-Dory* summers took place during Gull Lake's heyday, when it sported hotels, dance bands, float planes, boat races and swim meets. Dad appears on center stage when I visualize those summers, partly because I think it was the happiest period of his life, prior to the devastating loss of his brothers, but also because he genuinely thrived on family holidays and the challenge of making them entertaining for us kids.

Dad developed a habit of drawing up daily rituals at all our vacation spots, and the first item on his *Hunky-Dory* agenda was his morning constitutional, which his family of late sleepers generously accommodated.

"Mommy, I'm freezing," I whimper, padding through the icy cold cabin, rubbing the sleepers from my eyes, my arm curled tightly around Teddy. "Why is it so cold in here?"

I climb onto a kitchen chair, draw my feet up and curl into a shivering ball. Mother snugs a blanket around me and tucks it under my bottom.

"Daddy will be here soon," she assures me, returning to the task at hand. She has already logged a string of failed attempts to ignite damp kindling in the stove, a loathsome task that does nothing to improve her long-standing distaste for mornings. Gull Lake mornings are downright unsavory.

"Where is he, anyway?" I ask, certain only Dad can alleviate our misery. He has the power to vanquish anything, even rebellious stoves. My question doesn't really require an answer, because we all know where he is—he's in the middle of the lake, rhythmically pulling the oars of a rickety old wooden boat, blissfully inhaling his favorite time of day.

My only photo with Mother all to myself. Gull Lake, 1940

Then, just as Teddy and I and Mother begin to lose hope, he bursts through the door, all vim and vigor, and bounds into the kitchen, where he jams a wad of scrunched newspaper into the stove, lights a match and . . . the day begins!

After breakfast, the weather dictated the next event: Monopoly on the porch if it rained, croquet on the beach if it didn't.

"Set up the board," Dad calls over his shoulder, as he heads out the door for the pump to collect water for the dishes. "Donnie, you be the banker today."

By the time we unfold the Monopoly board, and our banker has doled out everyone's cash advance, Dad is back and ready to roll the dice. It goes downhill from there. Don has hotels lining

Boardwalk and Park Place in the first half hour, and we're all clamoring to "Pass Go and Collect $200.00" to avoid bankruptcy. Dad is not a good loser.

"Did anyone bring the Snakes and Ladders?" he mutters, vowing under his breath never to play Monopoly again. What a relief when the skies clear and we can play *his* game.

Dad was addicted to croquet, win or lose. We loved the game, too, but notwithstanding, croquet on the beach was no match for the fun of the lake itself. The trouble was, an obstacle course of croquet hoops blocked our route to the water, so we felt obliged to play at least one game, after which, we'd gingerly back toward the water's edge in a delicate attempt to spare Dad's feelings. He was now compelled to seek players from amongst our neighbors trickling down to the beach with their day's gear. (We noted no one else's paraphernalia ever included a croquet set.) I'd dive underwater in embarrassment at the sight of Dad waving his mallet up and down the beach in his quest to lasso a willing player. If a familiar face didn't show up, he wasn't averse to challenging a total stranger, willing or otherwise.

Actually, our croquet set traveled with us pretty well everywhere, and we were extremely adept at creating ingenious layouts to accommodate the terrain of the moment. We played on packed beaches, where the balls became so coated with sand we couldn't identify their colors; we bobbled about on dry, open fields, where luck got you through a hoop, not skill; and once we stayed at a mountain resort, where the only possible spot we could adapt for use, was a narrow strip of rocky terrain running alongside a rapidly rolling stream. The balls plopped in regularly, and downstream chases became a matter of course. I'm surprised my resourceful father didn't invest in a fishing net after the first day. The blue ball must have rolled all the way to Oregon.

Lunch was followed by Dad's exclusive creation, "The Hide."

While we were at the beach, he'd hide one chocolate bar somewhere in the cottage, then bellow from the porch, **"THE HIDE!!"** and our little herd of sand-coated waifs tripped over each other in the scramble to get there first. Mother and Aunt Lil looked on helplessly, as the cottage fell victim to each day's ransacking. I'm certain Don had psychic powers, because he found far more bars than his share. Not only that, he then hoarded them, alleging they were a wartime commodity, increasing in value by the minute. As if he didn't have enough of a nest egg with his chain of hotels.

We were comforted, however, by the assurance of a daily consolation prize. Once a week the local storekeeper made fudge out of her carefully rationed sugar, and Dad was always front of the line for a slab. So, after "The Hide," everyone got a piece of fudge, even though it was doled out in whisper thin slivers, precisely measured to last until the next fudge-making day. We used to try negotiating for our entire week's quota to devour all at once, but he would not hear of it. It drove Aunt Lil crazy.

After supper, the barefoot tribe followed the clang, clang of the croquet hoops back to the beach, like rats following the Pied Piper, aware that staying behind placed us in peril of Mother putting us to bed. We never backed out of a night-time croquet game—we'd play forever. Eventually, even Dad had to call it quits, and we'd clang our way back to the cabin to face the inevitable. But bedtime at *Hunky-Dory* was different than at home. It was an adventure.

It usually began with a trip to the pump with Dad for the bath water. He'd let me dangle from the handle as he pumped, and I'd swing up and down, crying for more, even as the pail overflowed. Then I'd take hold of one side of the pail's handle, while he grasped the other, and we'd slosh our way back to the cabin, with me grunting under my half of the load—a half he allowed me to believe I shared. By now, Mother would be fading, giving me hope that she might settle for a cold splash of the hands and face directly from the pail. I should have known better. She was fastidious about baths, and there was no substitute for hot water and soap. Today, I have to admit, there's no substitute for the memory of that beautiful, fawn-colored porcelain basin, filled to the brim with toasty warm water.

Cousin Marion, Me, Don. 1940

"I bet I can spit farther than you," Stan wagers, as Mother prepares us for the next task, filling three cups with water, and squeezing a sparing snake of toothpaste onto our toothbrushes.

"More, Mom," I plead, eager to take up Stan's challenge with a healthy supply of ammunition. "Pu-l-e-e-se!" I get another dabble.

We step out the back door, line up in formation, and brush—until our mouths can't hold another drop of foam. Then I nearly pitch myself onto my face in an effort to outspit my brothers. As an add-on to the contest, we also try to out-distance last night's spit, which spreads before us like the droppings from an overfed family of hovering crows. Brushing is never this much fun at home.

The last preamble to bedtime is the frightful dash to the outhouse in the pitch dark, with bats dive-bombing my head and my brothers spooking me from the night shadows. It's like being in a real live Alfred Hitchcock movie.

"Daddy, there's bats in my hair," I shriek, convinced they've clawed their way under the towel still clutched to my head from the outhouse run.

"Whatever makes you think such a thing?" he asks, running an assuring hand over my thick, curly hair in an effort to calm me.

"Stan told me bats like dark curly hair. He says when they land in it, they get all tangled up and can't ever get out. Are you sure there isn't one in there?"

"Yes, dear, I'm sure. Now let's get ready for our story."

Croquet, anyone? 1940

The closing ritual of the day is Dad's *pièce de résistance*, and he won't begin until the stage is set. He circles the room extinguishing the lamps, then sits before the fireplace, its glow casting his shadow on the wall. Then he begins.

Dad's amazing stories evolved in one of two ways. One was to let us choose a topic, and after a brief moment's thought, he'd be off and running with a story line. I remember him once giving my friend, Carol, holidaying with us, the honor of choosing the topic.

Smugly, she chose a tin can, certain this would stymie the shrewd storyteller. Before she could say Hans Christian Anderson, he was kicking a tin can into a plot so thick her head was spinning. She talks about it to this day.

His other story method was truly ingenious. He'd pluck, from memory, one of his favorite books—usually a classic—then revise it to accommodate our age, and serialize it into nightly installments, plotted to conclude on the last night of our holiday. Two I remember were *Les Miserables* and *A Tale of Two Cities*. Imagine wrapping up a golden summer with a Sydney Carton utterance even Ronald Coleman would have envied, "It is a far, far better thing that I do, than I have ever done; it is a far, far better rest I go to, than I have ever known." Spellbinding!

Exactly half a century after Dad performed his cottage rendering of Jean Valjean—candlesticks and all—I sat immobilized in a London theater, as the curtain fell on Andrew Lloyd Webber's *Les Miserables*. Without warning, a flood of tears suddenly streamed down my face. Dad had died six months prior to that evening, but at that moment, I distinctly felt the touch of his hand on my head.

Update:

Old *Hunky-Dory* still stands. It's one of the few surviving Gull Lake cottages to retain its original look and charm. I wonder if there are petrified Babe Ruth chocolate bars stashed in there somewhere? Don would know, but he's not telling.

Coincidentally, I married a man who's family also enjoyed summers back in Gull Lake's heyday, eventually purchasing property there after the war. And so, twenty years after my magical childhood summers, I relived them through our children at a primitive cottage we built on his family property. Little had changed; customary city essentials were still absent, and our own set of rituals ruled the day. Fetching water from the pump was a big event, and our daughter, condemned to two brothers as I was, knew the terror of nightly trips to the outhouse. Bedtime was still extinguished coal oil lamps and a crackling fire, but alas, my father did not pass his story-telling skills on to me, and our children had to settle for an unabridged reading of *The Cat in the Hat*.

The fourth generation has now arrived to an enlarged, winterized cottage we call *Hunky-Dory II*. It has every essential and a number of inessentials. Dad's silent, morning constitutionals unquestionably died with him. The last time anyone propelled a boat manually was when we ran out of gas while water skiing. My husband's idea of a constitutional is to pilot his ride 'em mower around the volleyball court, or fell a dead tree with his chain saw, then drag it to the fire-pit behind his all-terrain vehicle. A chipped and moldy croquet set hangs in the basement, behind golf clubs and horseshoes, and the original Monopoly board is buried under half a dozen editions of Trivial Pursuit. Yet somehow I feel assured that *Hunky-Dory II* is casting its own particular spell on our grandsons, as *Hunky-Dory I* did on me.

Sunday in Central Park; Dad & Mother. circa. 1928

Chapter 3

—A HISTORIC BLOCK ON THE BELTLINE—

The Beltline provided an interesting study in contrasts. A circle tour of our immediate block might begin as a stately stroll past magnificent mansions, the grand old sandstone residences of some of Calgary's most prominent citizens, then wind up before a row of ordinary stucco or clapboard houses belonging to the rest of us. Heading east down Twelfth Avenue from our corner at Seventh Street West, a string of unremarkable homes on narrow lots failed to attract attention, but when we reached the corner at Sixth Street, the imposing estate of pioneer rancher William Roper Hull loomed before us in all its splendor—1.7 acres or 22 city lots worth. *Langmore* was rimmed by a fence of green tubular steel that encompassed a dense barrier of spruce trees, creating a mystique that regularly drew us to the setting.

Heading south to the corner of Thirteenth Avenue and Sixth Street we'd encounter Calgary's first *selective* institution, the prestigious Ranchman's Club, a gentlemen's social club, patterned in the the style of British clubs. It too, had an aura of mystery about it because I never witnessed anyone come or go and decided it must be there just to look grand.

Across from the Ranchman's on Thirteenth Avenue stood *Beaulieu*, the grandiose estate of esteemed lawyer and senator, Sir James Lougheed, who hosted many notables of the time with his wife Lady Isabella Christine. Our jaws dropped the day our extremely reserved mother reluctantly confessed to having peeked over the fence one September afternoon in 1919 to catch a glimpse of the visiting Prince of Wales—the future King Edward VIII—taking tea in the garden.

West from the Lougheeds, the upscale Moxam and Congress apartment blocks paved the way to the splendid sandstone home of the Mackenzie Christie's on the corner, proprietors of Ontario Laundry. MacKenzie and his brothers, Nat and Stoney, came west from Ontario to seek their fortunes and indeed they succeeded—in spades.

Heading back north up Seventh Street toward home, we'd pass our closest and best remembered neighbors, the Dudders, a family of five children supported by hard working, devoted parents struggling to make ends meet. Mother sighed with sympathy whenever she saw Mr. Dudder heroically delivering groceries on his bike long after a full shift of driving cab. The neighborhood kids saw him as a different kind of hero. He was a semi-pro baseball player who regularly drew them to Buffalo Stadium—located where Eau Claire is today—to see him perform.

On the west corner across from us stood the President Apartments, where the only residents I ever knew were the Dudder grandparents, the apartment caretakers. Jimmy Dudder used to take me calling on his grandmother for jelly beans. She kept a huge pot of them in a cupboard, more candy than I'd ever seen in one container, with the exception of the candy jars at Bungalow Confectionery across the street. We called it Crystal's, after the proprietor, Hymie Crystal, who lived with his family in the back of the store. How I envied the Crystal kids engulfed in all that candy, while my dutiful mother judiciously rationed my intake. I never told Mother about Grandma Dudder's jelly bean jar. It was my secret bonanza.

Kids in the Hull

It was enough excitement for me just to creep around outside the Hull Estate grounds and peer in through the trees. For some reason, I always expected some momentous happening to take place, or at the very least, catch a glimpse of William Roper's mysterious widow, Emmeline, through the curtains. I was never rewarded with either. The best I ever got was a sighting of the scary gardener who sent me racing for home in terror. For Don, however, being on the outside looking in would never do. Intrigued at an early age with the trappings of the wealthy, *Langmore* was his opportunity to experience their world from the inside.

His neighbor pal, Donnie Dudder, shared his venturesome spirit, and first thing every morning, the skinny, brash pair put their fanciful heads together to discuss that day's adventure. The four directions on the compass dictated their choices: north to the tracks to watch for a train and wave at the conductor; south into Mount Royal to get lost; west to the Fourex Bakery to smell the fresh bread; east to the Hull's to fantasize and hide on the gardener. East, the hands-down favorite, won the vote most days. Through their own private opening in the trees, developed by repeated scramblings in and out, the boys would crawl into the grounds of *Langmore*, their hearts pounding in fear, as they scanned the yard for the dreaded gardener.

"Let's take off our shoes," Donnie King whispers, intrigued with the idea of a day's sleuthing barefoot.

"But the gardener will find them, and know we're in here," warns Donnie Dudder.

"Hm-m-m, you're right. I got it! Let's dig a hole in the flower bed and bury them."

Donnie Dudder sets to work at once, preparing a burial site

for the shoes, while his pal ventures forth to locate the gardener. Tiptoeing softly past the root cellar, the spotter's heart stops when the doors suddenly flip back, and the gardener arises from the depths. The chase is on!

"Donnie, dig up the shoes!" screeches Donnie King at the top of his lungs, racing full tilt for his friend, with the gardener rapidly closing in.

Donnie Dudder, alert, wiry and unrivaled at barefoot speed, even on gravel, unearths the shoes and scurries to safety in seconds. Donnie King is not so fortunate. Just as he plunges to his knees before the secret hole, a rough, muscular arm scoops him skyward by the scruff of the neck and unceremoniously dumps him over the fence, to the horror of his loyal friend, shaking in wait, clutching two pairs of shoes. Donnie King has some explaining to do to his mother that day, when he returns home wearing shoes caked with dirt—inside and out—and undershorts filled with a familiar by-product of fear.

Yet the Donnies were not deterred. There were other days. In fact, my brother even dragged his aghast, quivering partner right to the Hull's front door on one occasion, cheekily attempting to pull rank on the gardener by asking the uniformed maid for permission to play in the garden. The maid was so startled by the audacity of these barefoot waifs on the doorstep, she summoned Mrs. Hull to deal with them. When Emmeline appeared, Don was so taken aback with her common appearance—a dowdy house dress and gray hair wound in a bun—that he assumed she must be the laundress. Not until she convinced him otherwise, did he boldly announce his request, only to be denied, on the grounds there'd be no end to it if she allowed it even once. Insulted that his magnetic charm had failed for the first time in his life, he angrily turned on his heel and stomped off to the garden to play anyway, successfully evading the gardener in the process. To this day he brags about the afternoon Mrs. William Roper Hull received him at the door of her mansion.

Donnie Dudder's smiling face jumped out at me from Brian Brennan's *Tribute* column in the Calgary Herald one day in 1994—my brother's barefoot accomplice, dead at age sixty, leaving behind a beautiful legacy as "someone who made a difference." An insurance agent, he was described as "a quiet, decent man who gave—to his family, his clients and his community." His industry recognized him as the best kind of agent, one who put the welfare of his clients first.

In the Doghouse

Lacking the sophistication of my brother, the main attraction on the block for me was a neighbor's doghouse. One day when I was about four, I ventured out on my own to explore it. To my delight, the dog wasn't in residence, so I moved in for the day.

"Eleanor," I hear Mother calling, "come for lunch." Happily huddled in my new playhouse, I don't answer. I'm not hungry anyway.

"Eleanor! Come now!" is followed by the first hint of uneasiness, "Eleanor, where *are* you?"

"That's it, I'll play hide and go seek. This is the perfect hiding place. I can see her through this big knothole, but she can't see me."

I watch her circle the block repeatedly. I can still see her today in her cream and black houndstooth check coat—the one that refused to ever wear out—and hear her voice rising steadily as her panic mounts.

"Eleanor, answer me. Right now!"

Finally, unable to contain myself any longer, I spring from the doghouse, clapping my hands with glee at my cleverness, fully expecting Mother to respond with equal enthusiasm. It's immediately apparent, however, that her face is not registering glee. Angrier than I've ever seen her, she drags me home by the wrist, spanks me soundly, and plunks me at the table with orders to eat the lunch she'd prepared hours before—a soft boiled egg that has mutated to rubber.

The one and only spanking I ever received from my patient, gentle mother was major trauma for both of us. Not until I became a mother myself did I understand the probability that it was not rooted in anger, but in mind-numbing terror. Forever after, the event was a favorite source for laughter. I was frequently in the doghouse throughout my childhood, but never quite so literally as that day.

Happy Wanderers

I remained on a tight leash after the doghouse escapade, but Mother, confident in the presumed safety of the city in those days, continued to allow my brothers a fair amount of slack.

Stan liked to follow the milk wagons north to the Co Op Creamery on Eleventh Avenue, where he became a familiar face to the employees, who charitably allowed him to participate in their daily routine. His specialty was feeding the horses. Occasionally someone would sneak him an ice cream treat, and he'd skip all the way home wearing the evidence all over his beaming face.

If Don wasn't burying shoes at the Hull's, he was following the buses south up Seventh Street into Mount Royal, the neighborhood of his dreams. A favorite house on his route was the mansion built by the Dicks, survivors of the *Titanic*—the very Mrs. Dick that Mother had encountered in awe as a child. Don would casually and smugly assume the life of a resident, weaving his way into the depths of the area until he'd had his fill, then work his way back home by following the buses on their return route. Occasionally he traveled so far, he couldn't chase one bus fast enough or far enough to make it all the way home, so he'd sit on the curb and wait for the next one. The process continued for as many buses as it took.

We Three Kings. 1939

One day our neighbor, Mrs. Steeves, was visiting a friend in Mount Royal and spotted the strolling scamp. Assuming he was lost, she popped him in her car and delivered him home. He faked going inside, and after she pulled away, set off to complete the day's unfinished business. Another time he was gone so long, Dad became alarmed, and recruited the local radio station to broadcast a missing child alert. It was a lost cause, however, because Don escaped detection for hours, returning in his own good time by his own foolproof fashion. When he casually sauntered into the house, he was nonplused at the commotion he encountered and was especially astounded to learn that he was the cause of it. When our little Hollywood dreamer learned what had taken place in his absence, he flew into a rage. His name had been announced over the air and he didn't get to hear it!

Update:

When I circle the old block today, my emotions are bandied back and forth between the welcome sight of the thoughtfully preserved landmarks and the wanton destruction of others. Heading east down Twelfth Avenue my senses are immediately assaulted by a string of apartments that have greedily gobbled up every last house on the block. But it's when I reach the corner that my heart truly sinks to my toes at the greatest tragedy of all, the demise of *Langmore*. The Hull's priceless home was carted away in 1970 to make way for the Hull Estates high rise apartments situated there today. Some years ago, I visited friends there, in a seventh floor apartment, and was immediately drawn to the balcony where I leaned over the railing in search of the gardener. Alas, he's been retired. Don's dream playground is now a parking lot. The balcony did, however, afford me the sights and sounds of a spectacle that would have shocked the 1940's neighborhood: Stampede revelers stomping the night away on Electric Avenue in the next block. More recently, however, the avenue's electricity has lost much of its wattage.

When I start south down Sixth Street, dragging my feet over the unthinkable loss of the Hull's, the familiarity of the grand old Ranchman's Club at the corner begins to lift my spirits. (They lift even further with the knowledge that women have now infiltrated the all male bastion.) Turning the corner back west on Thirteenth Avenue, I discover the Ranchman's has spread its wings to encompass exclusive Estates Apartments on attached properties, giving that side of the street an entirely new look. But across the street, my heart sings at the sight of the Lougheed's princely *Beaulieu* undergoing an amazing transformation, involving a five million dollar, inch by inch, history-preserving restoration. It began in September, 2000, and is expected to take anywhere from two to five years to complete. The glorious gardens, after years of decay, have been restored to their former elegance and beckon Calgary's citizens to come in and sit for a bit.

Continuing along the south side of Thirteenth Avenue, the best preserved strip of my circle tour, I pass the untouched Moxam and Congress apartments, standing stoically side by side as they did sixty years ago, digging in their heels as if to say, "don't mess with us." On the corner, the beautiful sandstone Christie residence, home to the Red Cross following its period housed in *Beaulieu*, has been replaced by a larger building to meet the blood service demands of the community today.

Heading back home up Seventh Street, a small apartment has replaced the Dudder residence; a facelift has rendered the President Apartments almost as inviting as when they harbored jelly beans; and Crystal's Bungalow Confectionery clings to its corner, although for many years it operated under a new banner, J's Herb & Health. If I didn't know otherwise, I'd believe Mother had something to do with that.

Finally, the little stucco bungalow on the southeast corner— our beloved first home—gone without a trace. Didn't warn us it was leaving. Didn't even wave good-bye. One day we drove down Twelfth Avenue and it just wasn't there. My research indicates it disappeared in the early seventies (1972/73) and a few years later Stonehaven Condo's settled in, with Eddy's Nest Restaurant & Pizza occupying the ground floor. It's intriguing to me that the sites of Dad's first two Calgary homes became restaurants, the first by choice, the second by chance.

The Dick house at 2211 - 7th Street, of *Titanic* infamy, was sold by auction on June 28, 2000 for 2.2 million dollars.

Chapter 4
–GETTING AROUND–

Every manner of transportation rolled by our corner. The gasoline buses serving Mount Royal traveled up and down Seventh Street while the Beltline streetcars rattled past on Twelfth Avenue. Then there were the horse drawn wagons delivering milk, and for a period during the war when gas was rationed, Premier Laundry converted its delivery trucks to horse-drawns.

I loved the streetcars best, even though Mother thought they courted disaster. Passengers getting off in the middle of the street, repeatedly stepped into the path of cars navigated by impatient drivers passing on the right. Now and then, however, a streetcar enjoyed sweet revenge, as my brother Stan can attest. Early in his driving career, he drew up on the right side of a left turning streetcar, and failed to allow for its swiveling back end. Wham! He limped home sheepishly with a crushed fender.

The best streetcar trip of the year was the annual trek downtown with Mother to visit Santa at the Hudson's Bay. The weaving, clanking streetcar took on a whole new meaning as it rolled me toward Santa, who, unlike today, was the one and only genuine article. It was always bitterly cold, so Mother wore her fur coat, then disposed of it in the Bay's coat check, ready for an unburdened shopping excursion exclusively in the one store. She always carried a detailed list, and methodically went from department to department, crossing off each item as she made her purchases. There was no impulse buying. If a new dress was not on the list, you would not find her poking through a dress rack just to examine the latest fashions. Needless to say, our house rarely saw a new frill, and it was an occasion when Mother got a new dress.

The streetcars must have had a questionable braking system, because they inevitably gathered speed traveling downhill, and one rolling down Fourteenth Street West reportedly reached notoriety by working up such a head of steam, it flew right off its tracks and plowed into Crook's Drugstore. My family also talked about an incident when I was too young to remember, of a streetcar that inexplicably derailed, and veered through our front hedge late one night causing considerable damage to both itself and us. It was a major project getting it back on track. The same hedge was traumatized a second time by a Rainbow Cleaner delivery truck that mowed right through it and came to rest in the middle of the front yard. Mother gasped with relief that scant moments before, she'd removed me and my buggy from the line of fire.

One of my favorite activities was to place a penny on the track, then retrieve it after the streetcar steamrolled it flat.

"Don't you know it's a criminal offense to deface a coin of his majesty's royal mint," Donnie, the spoiler, warns grimly, when I proudly display my newly altered penny. "They'll send you to jail for a long, long time, you know."

"Mommy, Donnie says I'm going to jail," I wail, rushing into the house, wildly waving my definitely defaced coin. Mother can't make any sense out of my blubbering, so she summons Don.

"What are you telling your little sister, now?" she asks, resigning herself to another one of *those* days.

"I just told her it's against the law to deface a coin of his majesty's royal mint," Donnie bats his long eyelashes innocently.

"And?" Mother continues patiently.

"And, if you break the law you go to jail!" he announces all-knowingly.

I start wailing all over again. Mother deals with us both in her usual practical fashion, and assures me I will *not* be going to jail. It doesn't stop me from ditching my prized penny, or from looking over my shoulder for days, fearing one of Calgary's own might turn up at our door.

I loved the streetcars, in spite of Don, and it was a sad day in the early fifties when their tracks began disappearing, replaced by a tangled network of power lines strung about overhead for trolley buses. The trolleys were less polluting than fuel buses, but the need for power lines limited their routes, and as the city grew, they too, had to be abandoned. A favorite prank of trouble makers was to jump onto the bus's back fender, then swing from its trolley until it became disengaged, cutting off its power source. Then the pranksters would stand on the curb and split their sides watching the poor, cursing driver exit the bus, trudge to the back and manipulate the tricky re-connection. It often seemed they chose the coldest day of the year to pull this stunt—a day sure to intensify the driver's anger. I remember some drivers looking like they'd like to take these infuriating hellions and string *them* up on the trolley wires.

I also remember the day Dad came home from work bursting with the latest downtown news. City planners had made an unimaginable proposal for improving the flow of traffic; one way streets. The thought of driving down the left side of the street was inconceivable to him. "It won't ever work," he insisted. He eventually conceded to its favorable results, but not before repeatedly going against the flow in a serious attempt to prove his prophecy.

'319'
Watercolor and pencil by Joan Fedoroshyn

Chapter 5

–MOVING DAY–

Our one and only family move took place the summer before I turned six. We moved to Scarboro, less than two miles west from our Beltline address, but a world away to me. I didn't want to leave the only place I knew as home. I still remember the knot slowly rising in my stomach as the moving van circled our block, then shunted into position at our side gate, confirming the inevitable.

I trembled at the sight of total strangers carting our belongings out the door and up the truck's ramp. For all I knew, they were disappearing into the black hole of its depths forever. I panicked when I spotted one of the movers recklessly tossing my precious Teddy by a leg into the back of the van, the last item to enter before its door snapped shut and it labored off down Twelfth Avenue. The drive to Scarboro with my dad was pure agony, the actual move no longer the focus of my fears, but whether I'd ever see Teddy alive again. It would be my own fault if I didn't. Why didn't I speak up and demand personal custody for the drive? How would Teddy ever forgive me? How would I forgive myself?

We arrived at our new home to find the van waiting in the driveway, and when its door rolled up, out tumbled my fuzzy friend. I raced to the rescue, plucked him off the cement, squeezed him to my chest and braced for my new adventure.

With Teddy safely in my grasp, I was free to cautiously inspect my new surroundings at 319 Scarboro Avenue, and they instantly met with my approval. The MacGregor sisters were the first on the scene, sizing me up over the hedge dividing our two yards. Helen and Jean didn't disguise their delight in discovering a new friend their own age, and the feeling was mutual. Before summer's end, we had beaten a permanent opening in that same hedge and forged a friendship for life. As it happened, Scarboro's established, constant community provided me with many friendships that accompanied me from grades one to twelve and that endure today.

The initial drawing card of the new house, however, was its proximity to our beloved family living in the next block at 420 Scarboro Avenue — Uncle Harry and Aunt Lil and our three 'double' cousins: Marion, who was Don's age; Ritchie, my age; and little Audrey, a new baby. What could be more perfect than living this close to the family who lived so close in our hearts.

*Uncle Harry
and Aunt Lil in front of '420'.
circa. 1945*

A Palace Fit For Kings

I was dazzled by our new house, perceiving it to be a palace truly fit for Kings. As time wore on, I realized it was relatively unspectacular in spite of its whopping price tag of $8,000.00. It was a two story structure, designed narrow and deep to harmonize with its lot of the same proportions. A green peaked roof accentuated its height, creating an illusion of size. The interior was simply living room, dining room and kitchen, running front to back, and upstairs, three bedrooms and a bathroom following suit. The cramped partial basement was undeveloped, but Dad eventually squeezed in an extra bedroom, toilet cubicle and rumpus room around the washtubs and the enormous, belching furnace.

The house had certain features characteristic of the time, which are especially memorable to me now. There was a wall-mounted gas heater in the bathroom which was the nearest thing to heaven when I stepped from the tub all wet and shivery. I'd huddle before it with a towel draped around my back, each end of it held up against the wall on either side to trap the heat. What I wouldn't give for that heater in my bathroom today.

Right beside the fireplace was the door to a narrow, metal clothes chute running two flights down to the basement tubs, with an opening in the kitchen half way. We pitched a wide variety of non laundry items down it, either to time their falling speeds or test our skills at intercepting them through the kitchen opening. Then, of course, we took the ultimate step of trying to go down it ourselves by pressing elbows, knees and ankles against the sides with all our might to avoid plummeting uncontrolled to the basement. Friction burns were unavoidable, and I was secretly grateful when I outgrew the temptation.

Off the boys' room was an inviting mini sun room surrounded with windows, and it also had a gas heater which kept us toasty warm in winter. We often used the room for playing board games, and I still visualize its floor carpeted with Monopoly money. The sun room opened onto an outdoor porch, too small to be very functional, although I correctly assessed it to be the perfect size for a single bed mattress, and dragged one out to sleep under the stars one night. After a battle with mosquitoes at dusk followed by a dead-of-night cloudburst, brother Don, cursing me up and down, hauled me and my mattress back inside. So much for sleeping under the stars.

But the porch made a great sniper post for dropping water bombs onto unsuspecting victims below, except that Don's bedroom provided him with exclusive access, so he was usually the bomber and I the bombee. My friend Catharine had an uncanny way of getting under Don's hide with a steady stream of practical jokes, like the time she made our cross-eyed cat a pair of fancy, red rimmed eye glasses, with specially designed up-swept arms to accommodate ears on the *top* of the head. The gift, viewed as an insult to Smoky—and consequently to us—prompted the masked bomber to send Catharine a well aimed message from above.

Dry run dilemma ... frontwards?

I was jubilant the day I discovered I could climb over the porch railing, skitter down the roof below, stretch from it onto the extended arm of the clothesline post and swing to the ground. I didn't fully rejoice, however, until I'd mastered the sequence in reverse and knew I had a foolproof escape—and return—hatch. Cousin Ritchie used to plead with Dad to build a giant slide from the porch into the backyard, and whines to this day that it didn't materialize.

Stan had another brain wave for the clothesline post. The idea struck him out of the blue one day after school, as the two of us were digging into the peanut butter jar for a snack.

. . . or backwards? circa. 1950

"Hey El, I learned a new boy scout knot yesterday," he exclaims enthusiastically. "C'mon outside, I'll show you."

"But I'm starving. Let me have my peanut butter sandwich first."

"No, it'll just take a minute, honest. Then you can have your sandwich."

I follow him outside with his length of rope trailing, and he backs me up to the post, extending my hands around it behind me. Then he binds my wrists—with at least a dozen boy scout knots—and saunters back inside.

"Where are you going?" I yell after him, craning to see what he's up to. The screen door slams and all I can do is stand there and starve, wondering what's coming next. Two minutes pass, and his smirking face appears in the middle of the kitchen window, slowly chomping on a peanut butter sandwich. With lip-smacking relish, he tantalizes me right down to the last crumb!

It was finally my turn to laugh at this inveterate tease, the day his high school classmates hung him up by his belt on a coat hook, where he flailed throughout the lunch hour until a teacher came to his rescue.

The kitchen had one of those gas stoves on legs, with a high oven and the range alongside. The tea towels dried on a wall rack beside the oven, which doubled as a mitten dryer in winter. Underneath, boots were warmed for the next outing and Smoky curled up beside her dish of peas.

The rumpus room was barely large enough to accommodate our treasured pool table, a second hand relic that rested on two of Dad's restaurant tables, and slid into a specially designed wall slot when not in use. Its covering was worn thin and the cushions had little resilience, producing a dull thud with every bank shot. The pockets, clinging by a couple of tacks, were good for two balls—a third crashed to the floor. Added to our woes were two infuriating support posts which seemed to block every second shot. We had a miniature cue for managing post shots, but frequently still had to manipulate it to a vertical angle. And finally, many of the balls were blemished with chips and grooves which caused them to wobble about the table at will. The 3-ball possessed a crater the size of Grand Canyon. To our credit, we accepted these idiosyncrasies as a challenge, and became regular sharks at mastering the required adjustments—with the exception of the 3-ball, which could only be sunk by dumb luck.

The furnace seemed to fill the rest of the basement, and lighting it was an onerous task. Dad usually turned it off at night to save costs, and the first one up in the morning (him) padded down two flights in the frigid house to re-light it.

"I'm going to light the furnace this morning, Dad," I announce with authority. Dad seems in no hurry to perform his duty, and I'm freezing.

"It's pretty tricky," he suggests, "you better let me help you."

"No, I can do it myself," I insist, faking confidence as I head down the stairs. In truth, I'm scared stiff at the thought of this first-time undertaking.

My bare feet dance on the cold cement floor as I circle the furnace where it sleeps in silence in the darkest corner of the house. On tiptoe, I grope for the matchbox way up high on a makeshift shelf. I ready the long stick with the specially drilled hole in the end, strike a match, and wedge it into the stick. Then, with my heart in my throat, I creak open the furnace door, turn on the gas, and carefully direct the stick—armed with its live fuse— toward the giant burner in the depths below. The match flickers and dies. *Arrgh!* I have to repeat the process twice more before I succeed. But do I succeed! **KA-BOOM!** I'm sure I've blasted the house right off its foundation. For years after, I willingly choose freezing over lighting that furnace.

The previous owner of our home was a hobby gardener, so its most outstanding feature was its garden, especially the sunny backyard, notable for its profusion of perennials: peonies, roses, tiger lilies, bleeding hearts, lady slippers, lilacs, hollyhocks. The hollyhocks once grew all the way up to my brothers' second floor bedroom window. Up until our arrival, the graceful, curving lawn had only known the tender footprints of three sedate adults. What a shock it must have been when the new kids on the block viciously impaled it with croquet hoops!

A single car garage sat at the end of a long driveway stretching the full length of the property, with an ornamental strip of grass running up the middle. The manicured median effectively transformed it from a utilitarian runway into a thing of beauty, but alas, within a year of our arrival, the grass was chewed to pieces with our bikes, balls and hockey sticks, and Dad was forced to replace it with concrete. Knowing how much he loved the home's attractive surroundings, he must have made this alteration with great regret, yet to his credit, he did so without complaint. We pedaled up and down the new concrete guilt free.

The new surface provided a much better stage for our activities. It was clear sailing for roller skates and stilts, and the tennis balls I whacked against the garage doors enjoyed a much more consistent bounce—except when they hit the annoying door latch, which sent them laterally into the MacGregor's yard.

The property was surrounded by a collection of trees that I can still see, smell and touch. The lilac, apple and cherry trees exploded in the spring, and three giant spruce trees, regular home to a family robins, fought for territory in the narrow space beside the driveway. They eventually lost, and had to go. The birch tree near the front door, its one big branch stretching over the driveway just within jumping reach, was my favorite climber. I loved that tree. I spent hours of my childhood climbing it, swinging from it, or just curling up in its arms. I'm still in love with the memory of that tree, even though it stirs up images of scrapes all over my arms and legs.

Grand old poplars graced the boulevard and filled the gutters with fluff every spring, which I collected and stuffed into mattress and pillow casings for my dolls' beds. Being a consummate tomboy, however, that was about the extent of attention my dolls received.

Lastly, the house had a number of decorative gables and mini-roofs which added to its charm. The trouble was, pigeons—seemingly every pigeon in the city—found the gables charming, too. They nested in droves. We awoke to their cooing daily, and constantly peered through their unsightly deposits oozing down our bedroom windows. Dad employed every measure imaginable to discourage them, but to no avail. They were very attached to us.

One other thing that stands out in my mind about Scarboro during those early years was its gravel roads pocked with tire-crunching potholes. The roads were regularly oiled to subdue the dust, and until it was absorbed, cars and bikes left tire marks on driveways, and kids tracked footprints everywhere. Yet the area residents were in no hurry to surrender their gravel for the smooth sailing pavement cropping up everywhere else in the city, claiming it would only speed up the traffic. So, throughout my childhood, Scarboro had nice, safe streets policed by potholes.

Update:

I last visited my beloved '319' while enjoying a Scarboro walkabout with my cousin, Rich, in conjunction with the Sunalta School Reunion of May 30, 1998. The current owner generously offered us a tour of the house. I was saddened to discover a large addition on the back had erased our cozy upstairs sun room and its adjoining water bomb porch. On the main floor, the addition ate up the back yard croquet court, and a couple of small add-ons out the side—where the driveway used to be—had wiped out my tennis court. Its price had increased fifty fold.

Friends of '319'. circa. 1947

Chapter 6

–OPEN DOOR POLICY–

I don't remember ever carrying a key when I was a kid. The door was always open and Mother was always home. The neighborhood's only concession to any need for security came in the form of a hired commissionaire, who combed the area on his bicycle with his little terrier scurrying along behind, perilously close to the back wheel. We understood him to be a retired serviceman supplementing his pension as a watchman of sorts. Now and then he'd shine his flashlight up and down and round about, but he couldn't fool us—we knew it was nothing more than posturing to appear vigilant. If requested, he would commit to paying personal calls on his rounds, a service some women took comfort in when their husbands worked late or were out of town. We kids had a soft spot for the old gent, but scoffed at any need for his services and seriously doubted his capacity to handle a confrontation of any magnitude. To my knowledge, he never had to.

Mother, like many of the neighborhood women, didn't drive, but never considered it a handicap because almost every basic need was delivered to the door. The clomp, clomp, clomp of the Union Milk draft horse hauling the wagon down the back alley was music to my ears, its cargo of bottles clanging to the rhythm of the clomp. When the wagon stopped at our back gate, you could hear the milkman loading up his metal carrier with our supply; then the bottles jangled as he jogged down our driveway. We were such enormous milk consumers, Dad had to enlarge the chute to accommodate our daily demand. There was no such thing as homogenized milk, so when we needed cream, we poured it off the top, otherwise we tipped the bottle back and forth to mix it in. If we neglected to retrieve our milk from the chute promptly in the winter, it froze into a long tube of white ice rising from the bottle wearing a comical cap. Now and then a bottle would crack under the pressure, leaving a colossal mess of frozen sludge we had to chisel from the bottom of the chute. Occasionally a charitable milkman broke the rules and let me hop on board the wagon for a ride to the corner. It was the same milkman who had his horse perfectly trained to stop and start, unprompted, at all the required gates on his route.

Fourex Bread called maybe twice a week, and Mother's order never varied—whole wheat bread and nothing more. The bread man would appear at the door bearing a basket of enticing donuts and jelly rolls, but she never succumbed. She'd pluck out the whole wheat without the slightest notion of selecting anything else. A seasoned bread man would eventually accept the situation, leave his basket in the van and carry a couple of whole wheat loaves by hand to the door. Whenever the donut basket turned up again, Mother knew she had to break in a new bread man.

Once a week, Mother drew up a long grocery list, which she phoned in to Jenkins Groceteria for delivery. I used to giggle listening to her specify "fresh" for every single produce item she ordered, every single time, "Please be sure to send a firm, *fresh* head of lettuce; I'd like a stalk of celery, please, and please make sure its crispy and *fresh*; Is your cauliflower nice and white and *fresh* this week?" I used to wonder if they'd send last week's curled up rejects if she ever neglected to specify fresh. Once finished with Jenkins, she'd phone in the week's meat order to Fairley's Meat Market, and in a flash, it would arrive at the door by bicycle—fresh, of course.

The one other regular caller was Ontario Laundry, faithfully delivering the week's dry cleaning, which was guaranteed to include one of Dad's dark blue suits and seven *freshly* starched white shirts.

Occasionally, food was delivered in the other direction—out the door. I would arrive home from school to be startled by a vagrant standing in the driveway and Mother in the kitchen, busily making him a bag lunch. It wasn't uncommon for someone to turn up at the door pleading hunger in those days, and Mother was sometimes suspicious about whether they might actually be hoping she'd appease them with money, which would journey directly to the liquor vendors. She would not risk contributing to that possibility, and it was food they asked for, so it was food they got. When I crawled into my cozy, warm bed with a satisfied tummy on those nights, I'd try to imagine where the day's drifter was sleeping and where he'd find tomorrow's bag lunch.

Last, but not least, a faithful caller of a different sort was our pediatrician, Dr. Price, who would call en route home from his office to ease Mother's concerns over increasing body spots or escalating fevers. There was always a moment of terror when he spread open his black bag, and I wondered if he would withdraw the dreaded rubber glove, or worse—a needle. What a relief when he plucked out only a thermometer or a tongue depressor. His visits often amounted to little more than confirming a diagnosis of chicken pox, which Mother had already made, but we all slept better when he validated her remedies for our itches and wisely assured us we weren't about to die. I do remember him calling one day when we were all perfectly healthy. Mysteriously, he withdrew three needles from the depths of his magic bag; then Mother sat us in a row on the kitchen table, and he administered our immunization shots.

On two occasions, the doors of '319' opened to financially

struggling families of four, who took up residence in our scarcely habitable basement for some months. Dad hauled in basic cooking supplies and rounded up some army bunks, transforming it into living quarters of a sort for the grateful tenants. I remember the two little boys of one family bathing in the laundry tubs, and you could always tell which one had last slept in the upper bunk by the bump on his forehead.

We also had a series of short term residents, like the exhausted California family who spotted Dad out mowing the lawn one day and pleaded for assistance with their impossible quest to find accommodation. It was Stampede Week; they were hot, tired, and hungry; and No Vacancy signs greeted them everywhere. Before anyone could say Howdy Pardner, Dad was hoisting bags out of their car and assembling the trusty army bunks. I was thrilled when they invited me to join their family, which consisted of a daughter my age, for a day at the Stampede. We were all winners that day.

Chapter 7

—BEHIND CLOSED DOORS—

Dad, typical of his generation, was the authoritarian head of the house. He ruled with an iron hand, though never once raised it to inflict corporal punishment. He had the final word on everything, and more often than not, it was no. And no meant no, unless he was bent on a particular objective of his own, then he wouldn't take no for an answer. He was approachable, but unbending, serious, but funny. He had enough energy to run an Energizer Bunny into the ground, especially evidenced in his brisk, bouncing gait which added inches to his rather slight 5 foot 9 inch frame. He was a public speaker, debater, gardener, handyman, theater buff, reader, storyteller, jokester and dandy. He loved his family and his work. My inner camera captures him buried deep in the green, threadbare chair that he clung to long after the departure of its matching couch, book in hand and the grand old 1920's radio at his elbow.

Mother was calm, gentle, wise and understanding. She, too, was approachable, but had good instincts and the wisdom to trust them, which meant she could be persuaded to say yes. She was reserved and dignified, but not stuffy—she loved to laugh. In contrast to Dad, she had little energy, which in hindsight, was probably due to an underlying mood disorder which evolved into startling reality as time went on. I now wonder how many women of her generation, confined to the home, silently waged lonely battles with depression.

Mother's most outstanding feature was her mane of thick, dark, unmanageably curly hair which I used to love fingering into rolls or ringlets. She never went to a hairdresser, being adept at cutting it herself and secure with the knowledge that any slip of the scissors would be readily concealed in the curls. She washed her hair with Prell Shampoo and rinsed it with vinegar and it stayed bright and shiny for at least two weeks.

The one piece of independence Mother fiercely protected from her single days was her own bank account, which she'd opened in the dazzling new Bank of Montreal on the corner of Eighth Avenue and First Street West with her very first paycheck. As a child I'd accompany her there, tugging open the massive bronze doors and skipping across the marble floor to the circular bench in the center. She'd trust me on the bench while attending to business, which by that time, consisted of depositing the monthly Baby Bonus cheque issued by the government after the war for all children under the age of sixteen. I'd tilt my head back to examine the magnificent gold leaf ceiling, which could hold me captive indefinitely. Then Mother would collect me and we'd head back through the big brass doors, but not before she scrutinized the accuracy of her bank balance one last time.

I don't think Mother was crazy about life as a homemaker, yet she undertook each task systematically, patiently and thoroughly.

For example, she never strayed from her Monday morning laundry routine, which she ran with the assembly line exactness of a factory.

It began with releasing the door of the infamous laundry chute, and whump, our week's supply of clothes, sheets and towels cascaded into the tub below, overflowing onto the floor. Then everything was meticulously sorted according to color and stained items plucked out for pre-soaking and hand scrubbing on the wooden washboard. Now she was ready for the first batch of whites only, which entered the washing machine filled with water so hot they had to be fished out with a long stick. Next they were fed through the ringer into the first rinse tub—the bluing rinse—concocted by sweeping a small bluing cube wrapped inside a swatch of cotton back and forth through the water. The purpose of bluing was to prevent the whites from yellowing and it was miraculously effective. The miracle to me, however, was how it didn't turn everything blue. Then it was on to the second rinse and through the ringer for the third and final time before hanging. Each successive load followed one stage behind.

When the weather dictated drying inside, the cramped space in the basement became a hanging maze that took up every square foot. The sheets, thank goodness, went outside even in winter, freezing into stiff panels before attaining their all important sanitizing in the sun.

The final laundry task, wrapping up Monday, was to laboriously pull seven pairs of Dad's wool dress socks onto wooden stretchers so they'd maintain their size and shape. They came off those stretchers looking like they'd been pressed.

I have a feeling cooking ranked low on Mother's list of chores, though we never recognized it at the time, and loved her meals in spite of the fact that health won the nod over taste. Her unadventuresome repertoire varied little over the years, but we never got tired of her finnan haddie fish cakes on Friday or her Sunday roast beef dinners, and rejoiced when junket, jello or rice pudding turned up for dessert instead of the usual order of the day; fruit preserves and a Dad's cookie. We were ecstatic when she surprised us with one of her sinful specialties such as matrimonial cake, butter tarts or peanut butter cookies. She donned an apron for her first kitchen project of the day and it stayed on for the rest of the day.

Two supplements complemented our healthy diet; cod liver oil pills, dispensed by our school nurse, and Neo Chemical Food, a sticky, tar-like vitamin concoction dispensed by Dad. It came in a big brown jar and most kids I knew hated it. I thought it was better than candy. I remember Dad bending spoons trying to dislodge doses of that impossibly thick, gooey stuff, yet the time he packed a jar of it in his suitcase for a family vacation, the lid came loose and it leaked through his underwear and socks like it was water.

Mother was a beautiful seamstress, having mastered the art on a Singer treadle machine throughout a childhood peering over the shoulder of her mother, a highly skilled expert. She never parted with the treadle, maintaining electric "runs away on you." Each painstaking project took an eternity to complete, but it would be a work of art, whether it was a shimmering cape for one of Don's stage productions or my breathtaking grade twelve prom dress, a salmon colored strapless, heaped with a mountain of netting over satin. The dress project came down to the wire.

"Mother, hurry! Lionel's going to be here any minute," I wail, having impatiently zipped myself into the dress *before* Mother had attended to the final detail—the crucial top closure . . . DING DONG!

"See, he's here! Mother, he's here, and the hook isn't on yet."

"Calm down, now dear. Lionel won't mind waiting a minute, and Dad's there to greet him."

Chapter 7 — Behind Closed Doors

"But M-o-m, you don't understand. Dad won't just greet him, he'll probably interrogate him!" Just how preposterous my father could get runs to the limit of my imagination.

By this time, Mother is hard pressed to even get a needle threaded, let alone stitch a hook and eye onto the dress of a dancing mannequin. Yet somehow, she manages to secure me, and I fly down the stairs to rescue my hapless beau from the clutches of my father. If there was anything inauspicious about the conversation between the two, Lionel is a perfect gentleman. He doesn't tell.

My inner camera would snap Mother seated in the rose colored, high back antique chair, wearing a cotton house dress and a cardigan, mending underwear and darning socks with her black darning spool. There'd be a newspaper on her lap, but it would never get read. She stitched every night, a thimble seemingly welded to her middle finger, yet the mound of mending stacked on the little antique side table beside her never diminished. It was six inches high my whole life. The antique chair and table eventually made their way into my current home, along with her darning spool and thimble. The mound of mending did not.

Update:

Mother's Bank of Montreal closed its big brass doors in 1988, then reopened them in 1993 as A & B Sound. It's impossible to get used to its new status. A Spring 2003 face scrub has restored its stately facade to its former radiance.

Stan was a happy-go-lucky kid, lying face down on the floor reading the Saturday funnies, also referred to as the "coloreds"—the latest episodes of *Joe Palooka*, the *Katzenjammer Kids*, *Mutt and Jeff*, *Terry and the Pirates*, *Alley Oop* and *Dick Tracy*. But his hands-down favorite—and mine—was *Li'l Abner* of Dogpatch, and his hero *Fearless Fosdick*, a spoof on *Dick Tracy*, introduced as a strip within a strip. Year after year I wanted to beat that hair brained *Li'l Abner* over the head for ignoring the voluptuous *Daisy Mae*, who was madly in love with him. I couldn't wait for November to roll around, when maybe she'd catch him on *Sadie Hawkins Day*. She finally landed him in the fifties. For one period, the *Schmoos* dominated the strip—lovable, self-sacrificing creatures who experienced sheer ecstasy in dying to serve man's needs.

Stan had a black, wing-handled CCM bike that he pedaled full tilt everywhere because he was always late, even mowing down a pedestrian on his way to school once. The handlebars accommodated everything from his little sister, with feet precariously propped on the front fender, to his Calgary Herald canvas bag, loaded for delivery. The person he envied most was our own paper boy, Leonard, who could roll a newspaper and toss it with precision to every front door on the block, without ever stopping his bike.

Don fit the psychologist's profile of the middle child—contrary, impatient and unhappy with his lot in life. Dad nicknamed him "Monk Dimittis," and he was frequently at loggerheads with at least one of us, although Mother seemed to be his most understanding ally. He was born with tastes and aptitudes incompatible with the traditions of an inflexible school system, or the views of a puritanical father, and it caused perpetual conflict with both. But when the curtain rose on one of his summer stock productions, staged in our garage or Aunt Lil's basement, he fairly shone as he reined in his pre-curtain jitters and took command of wardrobe, lighting, sound and direction, as well as the lead role. The neighbors flocked to the performances, paying five cents for admission, and they most assuredly got their money's worth.

"Ritchie," I whisper, edging toward him at his command post, "is Mrs. Esdale here yet?" Ritchie is in charge of opening and closing the curtains on cue. But he's easily distracted.

"Of course, she's here," he says, turning his back on the director to slide the curtain back an inch so I can see the audience. "She's been here for ages. She's always the first one here. She's been here so long, Mom's had to make her a cup of tea."

It comes as no surprise to see Mrs. Esdale beaming from the front row. After all, we decided long ago that she was the president of the King Family Players Fan Club. We totter down the street in full costume to her back door at least once every summer, to entertain her in exchange for milk and cookies. It doesn't matter how good her cookies are, though, we've predetermined that it's *her* that gets the better deal.

As Aunt Lil's basement is approaching Standing Room Only, Ritchie is becoming excited.

"We're going to be rich," he exclaims, "the money dish looks almost full!" But who's thinking money? I'm wondering why I ever let Don talk me into the lead role of Cinderella. If I didn't fear a beheading, I'd bolt. But then, that wouldn't be fair to Mother. She's once again catered to Don's wardrobe demands, brilliantly transforming my pink Sunday School dress into Cinderella's extravagant floor length affair by basting a yard of matching taffeta to its hem. (I wouldn't dream of telling her I'd exchange it for a pair of jeans in a heartbeat.)

"Dim the house lights . . . raise the footlights . . . curtain!" barks the director. This is it . . . Broadway! The tomboy's performance is stellar, from the opening scene sweeping the cinders to the closing minuet with her prince, flawlessly executed with the grace of a prima donna. Don's exhaustive rehearsals have paid off.

"El, we're getting a standing ovation!" thrills the prince. "They love us!"

"So? Can I go now?"

"Don't you know anything? A standing ovation demands an encore!"

Ritchie fumbles with the curtains as the prince/director signals for an unexpected re-opening, and I'm swept from the wings back to center stage for three more bars— stupid, boring, annoying bars—of the minuet. "*I will never rehearse to this perfection again!*"

Don also produced and directed a game we called "Castle," the garage being adopted as our castle, with our neighbor Rick always assigned to the post of door guard. The rest of the cast consisted of a Queen of Sheba, a band of renegades whose objective was to kidnap her, and a King who deliberated over whether or not to pay ransom if they succeeded. The game was played in full costume, of course.

I was an easy going little kid with loads of friends—both sexes—two dolls and a teddy bear. One doll was coal black and the other had pink cheeks, long eyelashes and a glorious crown of russet hair. They were the same size and shared the same paltry wardrobe and equipment, but received attention only when one of my more feminine friends came calling. The rest of the time I was out scraping my knees on the trees or playing touch football with the boys in the park.

I adored my big brother Stan and had a love/hate relationship with Don. We scrapped perpetually—always his fault. I mourned the day Stan left home for university when I was just nine years old, leaving Don and me to do battle without a mediator. Stan never lived at home again, with the exception of school breaks. Don and I survived, and eventually even grew to like each other.

Life With Emily

Mother was a stickler for etiquette and manners, having memorized every word Emily Post ever wrote, I'm sure. A definite formality was observed at meals, especially the evening meal: the table was properly set, with cutlery, glasses and side plates in their correct locations; no one raised a fork until we'd all gathered, and grace had been said; no one left the table without being excused, and no one was excused until the last fork had been lowered. I can still see us glowering at Mother, impatiently waiting to be excused while she delicately dawdled over a half inch of pork chop or a thimbleful of potato. It's humanly impossible to eat that slow. Mealtime telephone intruders were requested to call back later, and outgoing calls were frowned upon any time between five and seven, in consideration of other families assumed to be sitting around their their tables with the same decorum as we. If an elbow crept onto the table or someone stole a dab of butter without the butter knife or, worse still, someone brazenly *licked* their knife, you could count on a subtle admonition from Emily.

Mealtime was a platform for social interaction, with the actual food almost an incidental. Conversation was lively—a challenge since we couldn't talk with our mouths full—and Mother, in a diplomatic whisper, would inject grammar corrections between etiquette reminders. Dad never gave up his British expression, "Give it me," and Mother never gave up her response, "No Horace, give it *to* me. Do you want us to give *you* to *it?*" Seeing this in print today, it takes on the air of a dismal endurance test, but that's far from my sentiment, probably because humor was always a welcome guest at our table and laughter not only permitted, but encouraged. I look back on mealtimes with enormous fondness and gratitude.

There were two persistent situations that forced Mother to compromise her table rules—Stan's trivial pursuits and Dad's post supper solitaire games. Whenever the family entered a heated discussion on some piece of trivia, Stan would dash to the basement for our *Books of Knowledge* and return with the answer which he'd read aloud between mouthfuls of mashed potatoes. Mother was tolerant of this disruption, recognizing it as worthwhile, but she saw no redeeming value in Dad's ritual of clearing his end of the table and dealing up a game of solitaire to accompany his tea. I loved it, and would keep one eye on the cards for possible moves and the other on Dad for slight-of-hand cheating, which I caught him at regularly. He claimed peeking wasn't cheating.

Responsibilities

We were raised with a strong work ethic and the expectation that each member of the family must contribute to the operation of the household. If we pleaded a shortage of time, Mother always responded with her father's favorite line, "There's all the time there is." "*Darn Grandpa anyway!*" I positively detested my Saturday cleaning assignment, and although sexism wasn't part of my vocabulary, I was fully aware that my brothers never had to crawl under the dining room table and dust the cursed rungs, and I resented it. For a period, I remember Dad drafting an elaborate weekly chart of all our duties, with spaces provided for us to checkmark completion of each task. We must have rebelled, because I don't remember it lasting long. Stan may have contributed to its demise the evening the dishwashing schedule stipulated, "Stan wash—Eleanor dry," and he claimed it read, "Stan—wash Eleanor dry." Bedlam ensued as he wrestled me to the kitchen floor and scrubbed me from head to toe with the dishrag as I kicked and screamed bloody murder. Then he released me, cheekily penciled in his checkmark and strutted from the kitchen.

From high school on, discussions concerning summer jobs did not center around *if* we would work, but where. Stan's never forgotten his grueling summer with the C.P.R., cleaning the inside of oil tank cars. It required a second day's work to scrub the oil from himself. I'm sure he considered it a victory to just get through each day alive, when dying of anoxia or heatstroke inside those stifling tanks seemed within the realm of possibility.

Don spent his most memorable summer with a City of Calgary gardening crew assigned to Union Cemetery. He wore a hat to fend off the heat, but went shirtless to acquire a coveted tan. Whenever a funeral procession approached, he respectfully reversed his attire, removing the hat and donning the shirt. We cracked up when Mother asked him about his day once and he grumbled, "Exhausting—hat off, shirt on, shirt off, hat on—all day."

I baby-sat regularly for a number of neighbors, earning 25 cents an hour, which doubled after midnight. My favorite clients were a young couple who always put out a whole plate of baking and a glass of milk, which I devoured seconds after they left. I never admitted I would have baby-sat for the shortbread alone. I also worked summers as cashier and hostess at Dad's restaurant, distinguishing myself daily with an intake greater than the till recorded. I assured Dad I wasn't ripping off the customers, but most likely failing to ring in all the chits when a line of impatient, time-constrained customers pressed me for prompt attention.

Carnegie Hall

We all took weekly piano lessons, but notwithstanding our love for music, were thoroughly undisciplined; after years of lessons, we remained woefully unaccomplished. Our teacher, Muriel Walker, was patient, kind and so-o-o beautiful. She held her annual spring concerts in the Palliser Hotel's Crystal Room. I couldn't have been more terrified performing in Carnegie Hall. Stan's claim to fame was a dubious First Movement of the *Moonlight Sonata,* and I once played a charming little piece from *Alice in Wonderland,* called *The Story of the Mouse* so fast my fingers tripped all over themselves. There was one concert when Don achieved recognition as Mrs. Walker's only student to receive a standing ovation. I still claim the kudos weren't drawn from his rendition of *Camel Train*, but rather his deep, flamboyant bows before and after, and his Glenn Gould posturing over the keyboard. Of course, it didn't hurt to have our Aunt Millie planted in the front row launching the applause for her favorite nephew.

Mrs. Walker scheduled the performances at her concerts

according to age, therefore, being one of her youngest pupils, I fulfilled my terrifying duties early in the evening. Then with my teacher embroiled in stage managing and my parents safely ensconced in the audience, I was free to run amok throughout the Palliser like *Eloise at the Plaza*. Of course, when the time came for the post performance presentation of certificates, I'd be missing, and Don would have to scour the hotel to find me. One night he found me at the top of the lobby stairwell dropping spitballs and screamed hysterically that I had "one minute to get to the Crystal Room." Realizing with mounting panic that I'd be in the first wave of recipients, I didn't dare risk waiting for an elevator, so I slid bannisters the entire way down and made a broken field run through the startled hotel staff that Jackie Parker would have envied. I arrived back stage just as my name was called and stumbled from the wings, flushed and gasping, to receive my honors from a bewildered presenter.

In high school, my parents moved me to Gertrude Taylor, an extraordinary woman, who not only taught piano while raising a family, but maintained her own skills with regular tutoring from Gladys McKelvey Egbert. The hope was that Gertrude might inspire me to greater heights and move me along at a faster clip than the snail's pace I was accustomed to. She was indeed an inspiration (especially when I found out she also played tennis) and she did move me along at an impressive clip, but alas it was too late. Having reached a time in my life when piano had plummeted to the bottom of my extracurricular list, I gave it up. I now reconcile all those piano lessons by periodically playing hymns—very slowly, and only if they're in the key of F major.

Chapter 8

–TALES OUT OF SCHOOL–

Sunalta Junior High School

I attended Sunalta School from grades one to nine. A grand old sandstone, built in 1912 from material quarried immediately behind it, Sunalta perched majestically on the lip of a coulee that defined the west edge of Scarboro, and was enhanced on the east by a long, sweeping schoolyard spreading into the neighborhood. The Elementary classes were made up of kids from three locations: Scarboro, which skirted the schoolyard, Sunalta, on the flats below Scarboro and Lowery Gardens, an enclave of squatters huddled on a flood plain of the Bow River north of the school. A fourth band of kids from Killarney, west and south of the coulee, joined us for Junior High. We all entered and exited Sunalta through our gender appropriate doors. I never went within a country mile of the boys' door in nine years.

Our teachers were all spinsters, since married women were automatically ineligible to teach at the time. Miss Elm, who taught first and second grades, was by far the youngest and left her position to marry—the only one to do so—following my Grade Two term. I thought Miss Elm was beautiful enough to be a movie star and I fervently wished she'd gone to Hollywood the day she gave me the strap. That strapping went down in the record books as the only one I ever received in twelve years, and I contend to this day, the punishment did not fit the crime—the innocent acceptance of a note passed across the aisle. After all, she'd only warned me once. Well, maybe twice. I remember her standing eight of us across the front of the room—seven boys and me—with orders to put out one hand. Then she raised a big, thick, mean looking strap, and delicately tapped each hand in turn down the line. I scarcely felt the strap, but oh, the humiliation of innocent little me being grouped with those seven thugs. A decade later, I would have considered it a badge of honor.

I used to estimate the combined ages of my other three Elementary teachers would have reached at least 247 years. They were s-o-o-o old. Miss Allison taught grades three and four, and if she were plopped into today's educational system, I expect she'd be making waves. Even to our young, inexperienced eyes, we detected her favoritism toward girls. If you were a girl *and* from Scarboro, you might even receive an invitation to sit on her lap, a practice I found especially disquieting when it was me she summoned. Compounding the unappealing situation was the feeling of helplessness to do anything about it.

Conversely, the impoverished Lowery Gardens kids seemed to receive scant attention. I wonder now what the school as a whole might have done to aid their battle for survival during freezing winters in makeshift dwellings by the river, often arriving at school without mitts or scarves and carrying meager lunches. In the spring, they were forced to flee to higher ground when ice jams flooded their refuge, such as it was. I'm still haunted by the shocking pictures of immersed hovels in Lowery Gardens that used to turn up in the newspaper. I don't know where families went during those times.

Miss Allison's field trips were something to behold. We always used public transportation, with our lone teacher single-handedly responsible for herding us through the day. Miss

Allison's approach was to pair each girl with a boy, and I'm still highly suspicious whether this mixed buddy system was implemented for security, or whether she took some strange pleasure in fostering mini-romances. I do know she delighted in her design and spent full afternoons drilling us for these outings. The exercise embarrassed us beyond words, but it still beat spelling.

Her regime began with walking double file to the bus stop, holding hands with our partner all the way, the girl boarding the bus first, and the boy joining her in her seat. Disembarking was carried out in the reverse, the "escort" stepping off first to assist the "lady" down the steps. Only when the ground rules had penetrated our thick skulls and we'd executed a classroom dress rehearsal to perfection—stepping up and down strategically placed stools and chairs to simulate the bus—did Miss Allison consider us fit for public. I mastered the demonstration in one take with the elegance of a debutante, but if Miss Allison thought for one minute that I'd repeat this routine in the outside world, I had news for her. At the moment of truth—on the *real* bus—I'd leap directly from the top step to the curb, landing with a thud at Sir Galahad's feet, avoiding at all cost the embarrassment of his assistance—which I did not need or want.

I remember agonizing over a pairing with my friend, Richard, for a field trip to City Hall, where Miss Allison had pre-arranged for us to sit in the mayor's chair—in pairs, of course. Richard, bless his heart, was a nice kid, but the size of a steroid-enhanced middle guard, and I suffered mortal agony at the certainty that we'd never fit in the chair together. The mayor must have heard my sigh of relief, when the first thing to greet our arrival to his chambers was his enormous, leather throne.

I doubt Miss Allison ever encouraged us to sit in pairs during story time, but she certainly didn't discourage it. Jerry sat in my desk with me one day, winning the favor with a two cent bribe. I accepted with two thoughts in mind: he was the smallest kid in the class, so I knew he'd fit, and I was dazzled with the purchase power of all that money—six jawbreakers. I don't recall learning much in Miss Allison's classes, except how to color inside the lines and get off a bus. And, oh yes, how to be fast at recess.

The schoolyard's only concession to play equipment was a generic set of two large swings and four small. In Miss Allison's class, I remember sitting in the row by the windows, which meant furthest from the door, and consequently, furthest from the swings. At the sound of the recess bell, I had to overtake the entire class in my sprint for a coveted *big* swing, which I often succeeded in doing. But my victory was hollow, because after half a dozen pumps, I got nauseated and had to jump off mid flight. But it never prevented me from racing to stake my claim the next recess, repeating the routine ad nauseum.

Also at recess, two knuckle-scrapers—hopscotch and jacks— were perennial favorites, as was jump-the-ball with a heavy lacrosse ball that bounced wildly off the school wall. And I wonder if little girls still skip Double Dutch to:

" Cinderella dressed in yella
   Went upstairs to kiss her fella
   How many kisses did she give?
   One, two, three, four . . . "
        . . . the counting continued until we missed.
   or

"Mabel, Mabel, set the table
   Don't forget the . . .
   Salt, vinegar, mustard . . . PEPPER!"
                    . . . pepper meant FAST!

Lastly, the most powerful memory of that class carries me back to the saddest day of my young life and a loss I never fully came to terms with.

It's a cold, January day in 1947, and I jump at an out-of-the-ordinary knock on Miss Allison's door. When she opens it, I can hear the unmistakable voice of our minister in the hall. "*I must be wrong*," I decide. "*It can't be Reverend Ashford. What would bring him here?*" Miss Allison steps into the hall, and a conversation takes place in muted tones. "*It's him, alright. Something is definitely wrong.*"

Miss Allison returns to the room visibly shaken, dabbing reddened eyes. "Ritchie dear," she chokes, "there's someone here to see you." My skin grows clammy as I see Ritchie stand and start for the door. My heart and my mind are racing full tilt, yet strangely, he seems to be walking in slow motion. Neither of us is prepared for the life altering news awaiting us.

I walk home from school with my friend Helen, as always, but I'm only vaguely aware of her presence, and her chatter seems to be coming from somewhere in outer space. I'm not registering a single word, because my mind is fully engaged in the daunting task of keeping an awful truth at bay.

When I arrive home, I'm not surprised to find my mother battling some similar obscure demon, except I'm soon to learn it's not obscure—it's all too real. Mother draws me into her arms, gathers her composure momentarily, then gives in to a cascade of tears. "Eleanor," she sobs, "I have some very sad news." She does not have to say more. I already know. I knew from the moment that knock came on Miss Allison's door.

Dad and his siblings had accompanied our Uncle Harry and Aunt Lil to Edmonton, where Uncle Harry had undergone neurosurgery that morning. The surgeon, Dr. Guy Morton, had reported successful removal of a brain tumor, raising everyone's hopes for a full recovery. Then the unthinkable happened and at age forty-six—the prime of life—Uncle Harry was gone. It was inconceivable to me that God would steal one from our warm, happy, safe midst. My precious Uncle Harry—I never got over it.

Miss Robertson; Grade Five.
End of term day at the zoo. 1947

Miss Robertson, our Grade Five teacher, was serious, scrupulous and utterly dedicated. She had a rather stern exterior, yet I sensed a softness beneath it, and felt comfortable and secure with her. She ran a regimented classroom, which began each day with the Lord's Prayer, roll call and health inspection—in that order. The latter was a tedious exercise in which she'd cross examine each of us individually on whether we'd brushed our teeth and adhered to our assigned bedtimes. One by one we'd solemnly nod affirmatively. Then she'd comb the aisles, desk by desk, inspecting hair and nails, while scanning the top of our desks for the presence of an item of supreme importance—a clean hanky. Mother supported Miss Robertson's health inspection wholeheartedly, being a crusader for early bedtime and an earnest advocate of clean hankies herself. I can still hear Mother's parting words that followed me out the door every time I left the house, "Have you got a clean hanky, dear?" I have a feeling the hanky business wasn't entirely to do with hygiene, but that she and Miss Robertson somehow attached it to honorable behavior, as if one would be hard pressed to stray with a clean hanky in one's pocket.

My two major accomplishments in grade five were mastering the division and multiplication tables and learning to write, each achieved through Miss Robertson's theory of repetition. Day in and day out, she methodically drilled us with mathematical flash cards until we could rapid fire the answers, proving her theory convincingly.

Writing repetitions consisted of dipping straight pens into ink wells and scratching spirals, line after line, page upon page, until whole scribblers were consumed with spirals. Once she was satisfied we were holding our pens correctly and the scrolls were flowing smoothly, we embarked on the letter A—pages and pages of A's. I had two goals that year: the first was to complete one perfect page of A's—or B's or C's—without my nib inexplicably releasing a giant blob of ink on my work in progress; and the second, to develop a penmanship as exquisite as that of Miss Robertson's. I failed miserably at both. I thought I'd died and gone to heaven when I acquired an Esterbrook fountain pen in Junior High, and kissed my scratchy straight pen and messy ink well goodbye. Some time after that, I remember Dad excitedly bringing home a sample wonder pen a salesman had delivered to his office for him to test. It had its own ink cartridge that released the ink through a ball bearing tip as you wrote. We all gave it a try and decided, "nah, this pen will never fly."

Miss Fraser, our Grade Six teacher, seemed to have a scowl permanently etched in her forehead, which made me think she either didn't like us or her job, or perhaps both. She fell and broke her hip late in the winter and I prayed for forgiveness for secretly rejoicing. I could not believe our good fortune when the substitute teacher turned out to be a man, young and handsome to boot. For many heaven sent weeks, we girls swooned over Mr. Schultz.

Then one spring day, Nancy, a dear sweet friend of mine, was playing with me in our backyard, and spotting our apple tree in full bloom, suggested we deliver a bouquet to Miss Fraser. I could never live with the guilt of refusing Nancy, so after school the next day, we cut a huge bundle of blossoms and walked all the way down Seventeenth Avenue, cradling them protectively from the swirling wind. We entered the Devenish Apartments and tiptoed silently down the hall, scattering petals in our wake like two nervous flower girls at a wedding. We came to a halt at Miss Fraser's door, took a deep breath and knocked. The unexpected sight of four eyes peering through a forest of apple blossoms dumbfounded Miss Fraser, but the moment she identified who we were, she welcomed us in warmly with offers of cookies and milk which we timidly accepted.

We examined her one-room living quarters as discreetly as possible, bewildered at the obvious absence of a bedroom or a bed. Tuned as she was to the minds of children, she quickly detected our puzzlement and, leaning on her cane, hobbled over to two large cupboard doors and folded them back. To our amazement, her bed magically rolled out! Nancy and I obsessed about that cupboard bed all the way home. The day was a life lesson for me, witnessing the transformation of my teacher from sour to sweet with a few apple blossoms. To this day, I never experience that aroma without seeing the faces of my charitable friend Nancy and our grateful teacher Miss Fraser.

By Grade Six, I was beginning to develop a social awareness (even without Nancy), and I remember two things troubling me greatly. The first was the appalling practice of valentine boxes, which ranged anywhere from barren to bulging, without any measures taken to ensure tender hearts were not broken. I now confess for the first time that my bounty in grade six was not the result of many suitors, but many valentines from one suitor. (Thanks, Arnold!)

Eventually, the inequity of valentines paled, however, when I encountered the honest-to-goodness broken hearts of my friend Helen and her family. It took Helen many weeks to work up the courage to share her private pain with me—that her parents were getting a divorce. Divorce? The only divorced person I'd ever heard of was that wicked Wallis woman who lured King Edward VIII from his throne. It was unthinkable for this to happen right next door.

Grade Six was also my one and only foray into the unfamiliar world of beauty pageants, my class choosing me as their candidate for Ice Carnival Queen. The term beauty is a misnomer, however, because it wasn't a panel of judges who determined the winner, but the class selling the most tickets. Never being one to waste time preening, and beauty comfortably out of the equation, I went to the rink the night before the big event, and joined a game of broom ball with the boys. I was holding my own—until Ed caught me with a savage backswing. The bad news is, my left eye puffed completely shut and turned fluorescent shades of blue, green and black, reaching a hideous peak right at carnival parade time. The good news is, my class came in second in ticket sales so their one-eyed beauty was a mere princess, not a queen.

Mother developed a curious routine with Misses Allison, Robertson and Fraser. She wasn't one to apple polish, and rarely engaged in the rite of afternoon tea, but every June she felt duty bound to invite the three teachers in after school as a thank you gesture for their year's efforts. I suspect an underlying consideration was the fact that all three were live-alone spinsters, who doubtless seldom departed from their hum drum routines. Tea day was daunting for all parties: Mother had to forego her afternoon nap to polish the silverware, bake some goodies and pull herself together; the teachers, none of whom drove, had to wear their tea finery to school to the scrutiny of bewildered students, so they could walk directly to the house afterward; and I had to strategize how to escape the whole disconcerting affair, as well as conceal it from my friends. I always managed to deceive my friends with an inventive series of distractions, but I was no match for Mother. Without fail she'd root me from my most elaborate hiding place, insisting I extend courtesies to the triumvirate. Mother's end-of-term tea carried a suitable idiom—it was nearly the end of us all.

Rushing home to do our homework.
Marj, Bev, Me, Liz, Mary, Jean. circa. 1950

My Grade Seven classroom was just steps from the Grade Six room, but as Simon Says, "Take two GIANT steps!" Elementary and Junior High existed under one roof, but were otherwise worlds apart. When I left Grade Six in June, I was a lowly little kid, and when I returned in September, I was magically a big kid. So what if I was the lowliest of the big kids. One of the most conspicuous distinctions between the two categories at Sunalta, however, was its slate of teachers. Junior High delivered younger, more vibrant teachers, and half were men—a welcome circumstance after years of antiquated spinsters.

Miss Hughson leaps to mind first with her bleached blonde hair, scarlet nails and tight sweaters—a regular siren! She could have gone to Hollywood with Miss Elm. The daily debate among the girls was whether or not she wore "falsies." We voted yes the day someone determined one was riding higher than the other. We only guessed at the boys' dialogue as they eyed her from their snickering huddles, but there was no second guessing Mr. Wilcox next door. He was an open book, chatting her up and down at every change of class, eyes coming to rest shamelessly at her chest.

And who would forget Miss Tyler, our art teacher extraordinaire, Miss Hughson's only competitor in the flashy department. She was a walking paint palette with her crimson Mick Jagger lips and gaudy, offbeat clothes. Her enormous jewelry jangled with every stroke of the brush, and crowning this work of art was a shoulder length, jet black pageboy with long, bold bangs that competed for territory with her great, gooey eyelashes. She was my stereotype of someone born at an easel— until I was assigned Mr. White's art class a year later.

Mr. White was the complete antithesis of Miss Tyler, quiet and reserved with a slight frame cloaked in earth tones. Yet it was Mr. White who introduced us to modern art, and covertly submitted my assignment to the Calgary Stampede Exhibition—a canvas of frenzied brushstrokes, applied in rebellion to what I perceived as a ridiculous art form. The following July, as I meandered aimlessly through the exhibits, my unmistakable Picasso leapt at me from a display board, flaunting a third prize sticker. I strutted all the way home, and never inquired how many entries the Exhibition received in its 1951 modern art category. Ignorance is bliss.

Miss McMurray, my pretty Grade Seven home room teacher, soft and gentle, was a big favorite among the girls. She became engaged mid term, and for the rest of the year our *Harlequin* imaginations wrote chapters to her fairy tale. When her wedding day rolled around in the summer, a cheeky group of us snuck up into the balcony of Scarboro Church to witness the happily-ever-after of our fantasy. Our hearts sank when an unremarkable, middle aged groom appeared, but we nobly consoled one another with the reassuring speculation that "he's probably got a really nice personality." Then our bride floated down the aisle to his side, he offered her his arm and turned to face the altar. At that moment, our fairy tale was hopelessly, heartbreakingly, irreparably shattered—Prince Charming was bald!

Miss Moll taught home economics, and my hatred for the subject admittedly clouds my assessment of how well I liked *her*. She certainly didn't win any awards making me wear a skirt to class, and if I had any notion of entering my father's business, it died in Miss Moll's first class. The assignment was stewed prunes, and I burned them—royally. It took ten minutes to create the pool of tar in the bottom of the pot and the rest of the afternoon to scrape it off. I also remember my cooking partner reversing the measurements for flour and baking powder in our biscuits. We should have patented that recipe. It would have made a fine Poly-filla for concrete.

The only thing worse than cooking was sewing, and worse yet, was the prospect of having to model my own project in the spring fashion show. Given the choice, I would have burned my grade nine yellow piqué dress along with the prunes. But given no choice, sewing classes alternated between painstakingly stitching in a seam one class and ripping it out the next.

"I hate this dress," I fume, pitching it on the floor. "Why do I have to finish the dumb thing when I'll never, ever wear it anyway?"

"Now dear, sewing just takes a bit of patience," soothes Mother, as if patience is something that will just seep into my psyche at her behest. The dress seams are in tatters, punctured with a zillion stitch holes.

"Patience be darned—this rag will never be wearable."

Eventually, I settle down long enough to piece it together, and after my compassionate mother makes a heroic attempt to mask the puckered seams with her iron, I hand it in. As far as I know, no one in the history of Sunalta School ever flunked home economics, so I feel assured even a dismal failure will net a passing grade. Now I just have the dilemma of the runway to deal with. Then two things come to my rescue; Mother Nature and my overworked seams. I only know of one way to conceal the frayed mess of a ripped-out seam, and that's to sew the next one wider. Needless to say, my repeated stitching has shrunk the dress—a full size. At the same time, Mother Nature is feeding me hormones, and I expand—a full size.

"Miss Moll, you won't believe this, but I can't get into my dress! I won't be able to model in the fashion show. I'm so-o-o disappointed!" *"Boo hoo."*

Miss Moll would never believe, that thirty-five years later, I gloried in sending my daughter down the aisle in a gown I had patiently stitched together, one perfect seam at a time—no size-altering rip-outs. And on the same occasion, the mother-of-the-bride heaved a sigh of relief as she zipped up her own outfit, created with her own hands—and completed before she outgrew it.

Miss Sherring, the music teacher, had a voice so robust it must have resonated on the moon. I won't forget the day it made a surprise visit to the city track meet at Mewata Stadium. Miss Sherring was posted at the long jump pit as a judge—supposedly impartial—but as I approached the board she had a momentary role lapse, and turned into a leaping, hooting Sunalta School cheer leader. That familiar voice added wings to my feet, but unfortunately, the judge was not willing to display further favoritism by stretching the tape. Sunalta did not place that day.

One particular room in Junior High seems to have engraved an odd set of contrasting video clips into my brain. I can see Janet sitting across the aisle and up two seats, busily preparing her desk for the day's class, opening her textbook to the required page, and spreading open her loose leaf notebook. Then she lifts the lid of her pencil box, and a scene snatched from *Friday the 13th*—sound effects and all—flashes before my eyes, unedited. Some evil doer had put a dead gopher in her pencil box.

I also remember the day a teacher with a celebrated temper pinned one of the guys—was it Ed?—against the blackboard and, using the kid's own water pistol, took deadly aim at his eyes and fired, repeatedly, raging at him to keep his eyes open. We sat in mute horror. The hapless victim never packed a water pistol again. Probably buried it with Janet's gopher.

I wonder if others were as troubled as I, with the school's preoccupation with tuberculosis that year, scaring me half to death with an endless barrage of chest x-rays, skin tests and repeated revues of symptoms. I had every one of them. Then in the middle of my fit of terror over having TB, the boy sitting directly across the aisle from me, inexplicably failed to show up for school one day. His shocking death from a jealousy stabbing splashed across the newspaper that night. His empty desk was a silent reminder of the horror for the rest of the term. This unthinkable deed had taken place right in my own neighborhood.

Junior High also delivered a new bunch of kids to our school. The nerve of this mob from Killarney marching across the coulee and invading our private domain! Barging into our classrooms and splitting up the tight little cliques we'd guarded for six years. It's difficult for me to judge objectively today, but I suspect the territorial barriers never fell entirely, yet I personally experienced a close circle of friends that included girls and guys from Killarney.

Finally, these were the years the opposite sex began taking on a new look, even though we considered boys objects of desire one minute and hopeless numskulls the next. In Grade Seven we girls awkwardly towered over them in stature and arguably in maturity, too. By Grade Nine they'd shot past us in size and began showing the odd hopeful sign in the dopey department. That's when I began sensing a difference in the touch of our touch football games, or when I occasionally elected to forego my trademark plaid shirt and jeans with the cuffs rolled up for something more feminine. It's also when I began to quarrel with Mother Nature, yanking a coarse brush through my much too curly hair in an effort to straighten it; dabbing lemon juice on my hated freckles to fade them; and cramming my (not so) "darling Clementine" feet into shoes a size too small.

Social mixers were introduced in the form of "shags"—after-school dances, which progressed to evening affairs known as "lits" in Grade Nine. These provided the girls with their first experiences in wall-flowering, and the boys their first encounters with outright rejection. Even I will admit the boys got the worst deal. It's one thing to grace a wall for hours, but imagine spending an entire evening mustering the courage to invite a girl to dance, only to be rebuffed with an insensitive "no," followed by a humiliating chorus of sniggers rising from the sidelines. (Did someone suggest the girls were mature?) Self esteems must have been dashed for life at those lits. I wonder if the shy guys who lacked the courage to ask in the first place were ever aware of their good fortune?

"Here comes Mike!" twitters the string of breathless flowers. Mike, the guy blessed with good looks on top of confidence built from years of elocution lessons, is inevitably the first to break rank from the guys clumped in the corner. "Who's he going to ask?"

"You, I bet."

"No, silly, can't you tell he's looking right at you?"

Fearlessly, Mike swaggers solo across the floor. As he gets closer, we girls face a conundrum: is the conquest of capturing Mike worth the agony of being the only two on the dance floor, stepping on each other's toes to the jeers of the entire school population? You'd think by now we'd know this conundrum exists only for Mary. He always picks her, and today is no exception. He takes Mary's hand, and she glides onto the floor with the poise of a pro—but then, she's had practice.

The Impossible Dream — Private Grade Nine Grad Party. 1952

The teachers finally introduced an inventive circle dance, designed to eliminate the scourge of rejection and fill the dance floor. The girls joined hands in a circle, the boys formed one that encompassed it, and when the music began, the two circles moved in opposite directions. When the music stopped, the person facing you was your designated partner. It was a great scheme—except it never worked. As might be expected, we all had grand designs on a particular partner, and when the music failed to deliver us to the feet of our fantasy, we'd shove, yank and all but dislocate shoulders to bring it about. And that led to the boys engaging in a full blown tag team wrestling match. Inconceivably, when the dust settled and the next dance was announced, we'd flood back onto the floor, and with renewed optimism, begin circling our prey once again. I don't recall whether I ever plucked a partner from one of those circles, but I do remember a very active dance floor.

Somehow I had the good fortune to slip through the pubescent, junior high years without the grievous trauma later lamented by so many of my friends. But there was one terrible Sunday morning in September, when my carefree days of hidden gophers, touch football and circle dances, was momentarily shattered. My experience with its parallel less than four years prior did nothing to soften the blow. My father's only remaining brother, our beloved Uncle Walter, was snatched from us by a heart attack, just five days before I officially became a teenager. My clever, vigorous, spellbinding uncle, only fifty-two years old—reciting poems one day, gone the next. I was stunned and heartbroken. I have forever mourned the premature loss of my two uncles. The gift of their lives so enriched my early childhood that I cannot help pondering the role they surely would have played in the years to follow. If only I'd had them even a little while longer.

Update:

The painful memory of my early school strapping was eased when I recently renewed acquaintance with John, an old Scarboro pal we used to call "Johnny," and he reminded me of the time Miss Elm voted me "best girl student" and him "best boy student" in Grade Two. I have no memory of this whatsoever, but I trust John implicitly. It's no mystery to me why she selected him, agreeably the smartest kid in the class, but her choice of me must have been guilt induced—atonement for that unfair strapping.

My last encounter with Miss Robertson was at Sunalta

School's 75th Anniversary Celebration in 1987. She was 95 years old and I was fifty. It had been 40 years since I last sat in her classroom, thinking she was older than Methuselah. If *her* math cards serve me correctly, she would have been a mere fifty-five. When I identified myself, she responded with great warmth, but only vague recognition. Then suddenly, her face lit up, she became quite animated, and reaching for my hands she exclaimed, "Oh yes, Eleanor! How are you? And how's your brother Donnie?" But she forgot to ask if I had a clean hanky.

In 1998 I attended a grand Sunalta reunion for students from the fifties. As I stood at the girl's door awaiting the bell—per instructions from the principal—I drank in the glorious vista of Calgary's downtown skyline. I couldn't remember a single building poking its head above the neighborhood rooftops when I was a kid. Later in the day, I reacquainted with my story-time companion Jerry, and reminded him of his two cent bribery in Miss Allison's class. He turned to my husband, who had just joined us, rolled his eyes and sighed, "Ah, but she was worth it!" At the end of a wonderful day, I brazenly waltzed out through the *boys'* door—for the first time in my life.

Sunalta School has battled the threat of closure due to a declining student population for many years. The Logos Society delivered a five-year reprieve from 1979 to 1984, operating a highly popular Christian School on the premises. Alas, a death knell was rung when an incoming slate of school board trustees opposed its alternative aspect. It returned to its former status as a public elementary school, and is once again fighting for survival as each new term rolls around. Sunalta is recognizable by its colorful mural, handiwork of Dean Stanton, waving at motorists speeding by on Crowchild Trail.

Lowery Gardens is now a nature preserve along the riverbank beneath the Shaganappi Golf Course. I think of my mittenless friends whenever I cycle the bike path that weaves through their former dwelling place.

Central High School

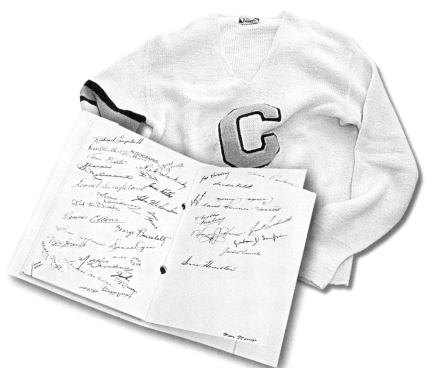

The summer of '52 closed the door on my nine years cocooned behind the sheltering walls of Sunalta School, supposedly preparing me for the next formidable step, but scarcely succeeding. Central High School was precisely 1.2 miles from home, an insignificant walk physically, but a major hurdle mentally. That first day of high school was a big event.

Calgary had four high schools at the time, three public and one separate, and many of my friends chose nearby Western Canada High for the technical courses it offered in addition to its academic program. Central was not only exclusively academic, but its principal, Fred Weir, unabashedly expected his students to capture the province's top marks and proceed directly to the honor roles of universities across the continent. It was a feather in his cap how many Centralites, in fact, stepped up to the plate to fulfill his vision—letting the rest of us off the hook! In the end, only one factor influenced my decision to attend Central; my mother, aunt, brothers and cousins had attended before me. Enrolling at Western would have been tantamount to a Kennedy enrolling at Yale.

And so on a crisp September morning in 1952, wearing the obligatory skirt and my first dab of lipstick, I headed down the hill for the somber sandstone on the corner of Twelfth Avenue and Eighth Street SW. Central, originally named Central Collegiate Institute, was dwarfed by its counterparts, Western Canada, Crescent Heights and St. Mary's, yet its castle-like architecture, combined with my first day jitters, created an illusion of size, which I falsely embraced forever after. In actual fact, Central differed little from Sunalta, other than I don't remember having to share my desk with a bucket at Sunalta when it rained. Separate girls' and boys' doors were carved in sandstone at both places, and the mystery of their origin remains a mystery yet.

In Grade Ten the separation of the sexes carried beyond the doors into the classroom, and I grimly found myself registered in a class of thirty-nine girls—all girls and nothing but girls. There were two all girl classes and the equivalent for boys; then if your name was Warren or Williams or Wright you were one of the lucky leftovers the principal was compelled to roll into a co-educational class. In grades eleven and twelve, he bravely scattered the entire alphabet to the wind.

Our principal, Fred Weir, son of a Baptist minister, reigned supreme over his domain, beginning with a strict dress code that excluded slacks for the girls or jeans for anyone. (I can't even imagine spiked hair or body piercings on the same planet with Mr. Weir.) Central's cheerleaders held no resemblance to the Dallas Cowgirls, but their classy mid-calf pleated skirts never dampened their enthusiasm. There was no smoking, bad language, or romantic hand holding on the school premises or within sight of it. And parents endorsed all the rules.

Mr. Weir retired at age sixty-five at the end of my grade ten year, and tragically died a few months later. The week following his death, our minister, Dr. Parsons, focused his sermon on Mr. Weir's beautiful garden in Scarboro, reminding us how his secluded back yard was as carefully tended as his visible front yard, suggesting this was the example Mr. Weir set for his own life–scrupulous inside and out. It became my lasting legacy of him. The cheerleaders' respect was not so lasting. Their hemlines remained at the modest, mid-calf length for exactly one year following his death, then shot to the top of their thighs.

My brothers had prepared me in advance for most of my teachers, so I arrived at Central with a litany of preconceived notions. My first strategy was to steer clear of Jessie Maxwell's French class because she'd flunked both of them. Faced with having to take a language, I headed directly to Ingvar Gislason's Latin class, where I scraped through by the skin of my teeth all three years. I seriously doubt I'd have fared any worse at French.

Mr. Gislason's habit each day was to send a row at a time to the blackboard to write the previous day's assignment of sentence translations, and I was eternally grateful he never once diverted from this routine. I sat in the sixth seat in my row, so declared the sixth sentence my only required homework. (Dr. Parson's backyard sermon was briefly lost on me.) Of course, if I arrived in class to discover an absentee in my row, I was dead in the woods.

There were two teachers who had preconceived notions of

me, the first being Nellie James, a physical education teacher who assumed I carried the athletic genes of my cousin Marion preceding me, and repeatedly placed me front row center in the gym with instructions to the class to "follow Eleanor." What a relief it never got more complicated than jumping jacks. The second was Hilda Hobbs, who'd been a school mate of my mother's in the dark ages, and nursed the expectation that I would bring my mother's academic excellence to her social studies class. She even phoned Mother one day when test results clearly indicated otherwise. I was probably my father's daughter that day.

I suspect the imposing figure and fearsome glare of J. Winston Churchill, the physics teacher, ranks up there in the memories of all Centralites. His glare always seemed to be directed at more than one of us at a time, which, combined with his habit of muddling names, occasionally provided comic relief. It brought down the house the day he rebuked Lionel Singleton for answering a question directed at Alan Shelwick. "Not you, Shellington," he railed, "I asked Singlewick!"

Mr. Churchill stressed maintaining a perfect set of notes, which he never modified throughout his career, making brother Don's notes—passed down to him from a friend—conveniently usable for me. I had to copy them in my own hand, mind you, because Mr. Churchill had checked and stamped every single page "Accepted JWC." I liked physics and enjoyed reasonable grades. Don flunked, in spite of his great notes.

And who could forget Mr. Churchill's penalty for disturbers: a hand written copy of the poem *The Diverting History of John Gilpin*, which had little to do with physics, but everything to do with its substantial length (252 lines), and the fact that its lines fit conveniently on the width of a standard sheet of foolscap, providing him easy verification that we hadn't fudged the assignment. Considering the number of times I wrote that poem, it's almost inconceivable that I can only remember the two opening lines:

> "John Gilpin was a citizen
> Of credit and renown . . . ."

Mr. Churchill won my affection in grade twelve, however, when he could not hide his pride in our basketball, football and track teams scooping the interscholastic trophies. Considering the size of Central, it was like Canada stealing gold from the U.S. Our rivals were reluctantly resigned to Central's brainy nerds prevailing academically, but they were pretty steamed when we triumphed in the sports arena. Our gloating Mr. Churchill turned into Don Cherry for a day as he stood before our school assembly, ranting on about Crescent and Western bursting through the gates of Mewata Stadium with banners flying, cheer leaders leaping and bands blaring. Then, lowering his voice to an anguished whisper, he lamented, "Poor, pathetic, underpopulated Central—no fanfare at all. We arrived with only one thing—a track team!" The auditorium rocked.

Sid Jones, my math teacher, apparently collaborated on our text book, yet he frequently didn't seem to have a clue about its content. When solicited for help with a problem, he'd open the book at the page in question, lean up against my front row desk and silently rock back and forth, back and forth, as he stared unblinking at the page. After interminable rocking, he'd finally raise his head and call on Don, the class genius for the answer, which Don had calculated in the first fifteen seconds. I also remember math class being my last of the morning when my empty stomach chronically voiced its displeasure. (Mother always said I should eat breakfast.) It was pure hell trying to silence the embarrassing rumblings for a full forty minutes every day with Mr. Jones rocking at my toes.

Mae Powell, the teeny tiny music teacher, was the complete antithesis of the ample bodied Miss Sherring of Sunalta. Yet I remember both music teachers for activities outside the classroom. Miss Powell lived in an apartment just west of the school which was on my walking route, and on the rare occasion I reached her place early enough, my day would start with a chuckle over her bicycle routine. It began with all ninety pounds of her straining to wrestle her cumbersome set of wheels down the front steps of her apartment where she steadfastly housed it every night. Then looking for all the world like Dorothy with a basketful of Toto, she'd pedal the one short block to the school, where she'd dismount and lug the heavy bike up the school steps for safekeeping inside. My guess is she got a better burn hauling that bike than pedaling it, but for sure, it was never stolen.

Central acquired two new teachers during our tenure, which caused quite a stir among the students, and no doubt among the staid, vintage teachers as well. Both were men, slight of stature and younger than the others, but the similarity ended there. Len Harper was a self-professed Christian, eager to share the good news with his classes, but his bible readings occasionally touched off near uprisings, especially among our considerable Jewish population. Cy Groves was British, Jewish, a bit of a maverick, and at twenty-six years of age, entering only his second year in the classroom. Unfortunately for these rookies, we placed them in a separate category from our seasoned teachers and treated them with alarming irreverence. It would have been unthinkable to plant a shriek bomb on the cylinder head of Mr. Churchill's car, but not unthinkable for George and Scott to do such a thing to our long suffering Mr. Harper.

"What's going on?" I ask Lois, as we begin our after school walk home. "Why are those guys hanging out by the teachers' parking lot?"

"Something must be up. Let's go see." We join the gang lurking about the teachers' cars. "What's going on you guys?"

Everyone gives us the same reply, "Don't go away. You gotta see this!" Their body language adds volumes to their intriguing invitation, so we stay.

As one teacher after another arrives at his car, the demeanor of the boys doesn't change, but when Mr. Harper approaches— end of day nerves frazzled, as always—they become noticeably animated. Every guy in the parking lot is hyperventilating as they watch him slide into the driver's seat and turn the key. Then they stop breathing altogether. Very soon, a low wail erupts under the hood, rapidly intensifying until it reaches a shrill screech. The color drains from Mr. Harper's face and he grips the steering wheel with such ferocity, I think he's about to wrench it from its column. He remains frozen in this posture until the screeching culminates in a deafening explosion, which propels him from his vehicle, the poor man's face registering sheer terror as he flees back into the school.

It was days before we saw Mr. Harper again, and then only briefly, before he disappeared for good. It would not surprise me to learn he suffered permanently from post traumatic stress disorder following that unconscionable act.

I have less sympathy for our young maverick whose unrestrained manner was a clear contradiction to a school steeped in the rigid code of a preacher's son. As one might expect, we viewed his free spirit as our license to cut loose, and very quickly things spun out of control. In desperation he launched a series of punishments, which steadily escalated to outrageous proportions. Inevitably, the day came when they boiled over, and as luck would have it, the guy least likely to create a disturbance became the victim of his wrath. In exasperated fury, our tormented professor imposed an impossible penalty on an unbelieving Morris—better known as "Moose"— "to hand write five copies of *Julius Caesar* (maybe it was just Act I) before English class the following day"—an all nighter, pure and simple. Unless you have help.

That evening a group of Moose's friends banded together and turned the preposterous assignment into a party, operating on the premise that many hands—and many carbons—make light work. The fourth carbon copies were indeed *light*, in fact, barely legible, but since the assignee's objective was clearly quantity as opposed to quality, the group voted them valid. The following day, Moose, backed by his impertinent, smirking accomplices, flopped the mountainous, multi-scripted production on the desk of our aghast teacher. The look on his face was worth every agonizing case of writer's cramp, and we all fell out of our desks in hysterics. The exercise designed to restore order collapsed into chaos.

The Social Scene

Frats and sororities were not sanctioned by the school, but were allowed the freedom to operate at arm's length. I made my first brave anti-discrimination statement by turning down my invitations to join, in homage to friends inexplicably excluded, which I viewed as incongruous to the whole meaning of a sisterhood. I confess I did it with a twinge of anxiety about the possible consequence of being banished from society, but to my relief, I wasn't.

The sororities and frats were an integral part of the social scene in high school just the same, often initiating house parties and major dances. They also provided logo pins, looked upon as a favorable item for going steady, although not absolutely essential. Accepting and wearing a boy's frat pin wasn't a lifetime commitment as panic-stricken parents fretted, but it did broadcast an agreement of exclusive dating rights. The Monday morning chatter often revolved around who got "pinned" on the weekend, and by whom, as we examined everyone's sweaters for clues. "Did you see the Tau Eta Nu pin Joan's wearing? Who's the guy?" For some, going steady was a fairly serious event, while for others, it was little more than the previous weekend's conquest— a new backdrop for a roving pin.

I remember vacillating over accepting my steady boyfriend's pin, wondering if it was worth the inevitable confrontation with my parents. The fact that they were very fond of Lionel did nothing to allay their fears of this unfamiliar rite. Well, he did what any impatient young charmer would do—he offered it to another girl, who accepted it without deliberation. As I recall the story, however, she returned it within the week with about as much fanfare as she'd received it. But I wasn't about to risk losing him again, so I accepted his second offer smartly, popped his Eta Beta Pi pin onto my sweater and gamely faced my parents . . . who fainted dead away as I knew they would. When they regained consciousness, I calmed them down with an assurance that Lionel and I were *not* going to run off and get married. And we never did.

Of course, dating for me was an exercise in management with or without a pin, considering my father would have preferred to padlock me to the piano. I can remember our house being the only one on the block with its outdoor light on late at night, a luminous beacon radiating from one end of Scarboro Avenue to the other. Whenever a date lost his bearings bringing me home after dark, I'd point and mumble, "It's the house with the light on." It was quickly adopted as a catch-phrase for much teasing, "Let me guess. I bet it's the house with the light on."

One night when returning well past curfew, and feverishly plotting my strategy for sneaking in undetected, I instructed my friend Dennis not to drive up the floodlit driveway, and risk waking my parents in the bedroom above. I had no sooner issued the order, when he screeched up the drive, jammed on the brakes, revved the motor, stuck his head out the window and hollered— loud enough to wake the dead—"Mr. King, here's your wayward daughter!" Then he rolled me out of the car and drove off down the street laughing his fool head off. I reacted appropriately by collapsing in hysterics on the front steps. My father? He rose to the occasion by placing his faith in this yokel whose conscience was so clean, he was willing to broadcast—to the entire neighborhood—the late delivery of his daughter. Dad peeled me from the steps without a word. Scooped from the stoop, again!

The grandest social event of the school year was the Big Three Ball, an impressive, three sorority affair I remember attending in the fairy tale setting of the Bowness Golf and Country Club on the bluff overlooking Bowness Park. The guys were regular Prince Charmings in their suits and ties, and we girls were Cinderellas for a night in our strapless gowns and corsages—except this Cinderella's feet screamed bloody murder in her glass slippers.

Dance cards were presented on arrival, and the hapless guys were assigned the onerous task of getting them filled. They'd circulate among their buddies, half-heartedly attempting to negotiate deals through offers to reciprocate. The real hustlers had their cards filled before the first dance, an impressive achievement, except the signatures on the cards didn't always translate to the dance floor. In fact, many signees were masters at escaping their obligations. Could they help it if the band struck the opening chord for a dance at the very moment they planned a cigarette break? If you had a watchful date, he'd fill in for the deserter, if not, you joined the other rejects forsaken by their puffing partners. Sometimes I think we found that preferable.

Our favorite school events were the Friday night dances

which followed the basketball games. We enjoyed the ones on our own turf best, and if they followed a win, we bounced off the walls. The jive was the *in* dance and few of us swooned over Bill Haley—with his goofy lock of hair pasted on his forehead—or his Comets, but we were wild about their music; *Rock Around the Clock* and *ABC Boogie*. The auditorium also shook to *Sh-Boom* and *Wimoweh*, nonsensical titles made popular by the Crew Cuts and the Weavers, now enjoying a revival. We slowed the pace for Nat King Cole's *Mona Lisa*, The Penguins' *Earth Angel*, The Platters' *Only You* and the Four Aces pleading *Tell Me Why*. At some point in the evening, the Mills Brothers inevitably turned up with their *Glow Worm*, and a snake would form as we bunny hopped around the auditorium, pounding the floor mercilessly. Day in and day out Patti Page asked *How Much is the Doggie in the Window?* and Rosie Clooney sent an invitation to *Come On-a My House,* while Chuck Berry screeched for *Maybelline*. We laughed when Johnny Ray—backed by the Four Ladds—thrashed on the floor under *The Little White Cloud That Cried,* and cried when Eddie Fisher whimpered *Oh! My Papa*. In the meantime, Elvis Presley, a struggling unknown, was making his first nervous stage appearance in Memphis, Tennessee, his shaking left leg revealing an uncontrollable case of nerves throughout the entire performance. Someone determined the girls were responding to the leg as much as the music, and the rest is history. We had to wait two years to see the future legend, and even then, were denied the leg—and the pelvis. The Ed Sullivan camera crew judiciously chopped Elvis off at the waist.

Graduation carried little of the hype surrounding the occasion today—no all night parties, no linen and crystal dinners, no tuxes or limos. Not even caps and gowns. Basic exercises were held in the school's hot, crowded gymnasium, as was the dance. But we thought both occasions were grand. Our teachers urged everyone to attend the dance, with or without partners, but many of the kids were narrow minded enough to believe a date was imperative, and that unfortunately resulted in some remaining home. I won't forget one sensitive teacher taking a subtle stab at providing her own personal dating service, but it failed entirely. (I'm loathe to admit that anything's an improvement today, but that is one situation that is.)

Preparing for the dance was complicated, since I deemed it critical to have a tan on my face, neck and shoulders to complement my strapless gown. How was I to know the golden beauty on the sunlamp box was a lie?

Graduation Day.
Grade 12. 1955

"I've been under this lamp every night for five days now, and I don't look anything like her," I moaned, monitoring myself in the mirror every five minutes. I was used to turning deep bronze within days of exposure to the summer sun. Rapidly running out of time, there was only one thing to do. Each session, I moved the sunlamp closer—for a longer period.

Fortunately, my face, toughened by at least some year round exposure, weathered the attack with little more than a severe case of the tingles, but my chest rebelled with a blanket of angry blisters that festered for days on a screaming bed of hot coals. As Mother stitched that final hook on my dress, and Lionel rang the doorbell, each mini-Vesuvius was erupting. It goes without saying, a third degree chest and a salmon pink strapless gown, layered with mounds of stiff, abrasive netting is a formula for an evening from hell. Tears rolled from my eyes as well as my chest, and if Lionel harbored any dream of slow dancing, he was compelled to dream on. My dream was to get home, tear off my clothes, and plunge into a tub of ice cubes.

Fads and Fashions

The kids at Central were very fashion conscious, although many of us did not have budgets to fit our tastes. The boys wore mostly cords or cottons twills with v-necked lambswool sweaters. Brother Don, the family fashion plate, shopped for his wardrobe at The English Shop, the most exclusive store in town, located on Eighth Avenue between First Street West & Centre, a shop that exuded grandeur with its exquisite oak floors and cabinets. His closet held every shade of sweater in the Alan Payne collection, and he became an expert at washing and blocking them himself, as well as ironing his own shirts. Not even Martha Stewart could have met his standard of perfection. He maintained his perfectly coifed hair in a stiff pompadour with Hollywood Wave Set, a green goo much like today's styling gels. Apparently if your hair was fair, it had a tendency to turn it green, so some guys resorted to sugar and water to lock in their locks.

Although jeans were banned at school, they were the established garb for weekends. Don would purchase a snug fitting pair, put them on as soon as he got home and direct me to hose him down in the backyard. Then he'd lie in the sun until they shrank to form fitting perfection. It was an assignment I relished, although it took every ounce of willpower to resist dismantling his Hollywood pompadour, an act that would have spelled certain death.

Only once do I recall specific colors becoming a fashion trend, and that was the pink and charcoal period for the guys—pink shirts worn with charcoal pants and sweaters. One day in math class, Mr. Jones took up his familiar mute, rocking posture in front of my desk, and slowly scanned the sea of pink and charcoal before him. After an even longer than usual period of bewildering silence, he deadpanned, "Where's the sale?" And to think I never believed he possessed a shred of humor!

We girls wore cashmere or lambswool sweaters over long wool skirts reaching just above our bobby sox. The outfit was topped with either a round dickey collar or a colorful Liberty scarf. I admired my friend Lois's cashmere sweaters with envy, but could never aspire to owning one. It took me weeks of baby-sitting to save up for a new lambswool, which I always bought at the Bay. I rarely stepped foot in the popular Ted McGregor's on First Street or Don's favorite English Shop. Kilts were extremely popular and I had a green plaid one with a large, decorative pin that was a favorite. My most cherished skirt, however, was a straight cut navy blue with a double kick pleat in the back. I was the cock of the walk in that skirt.

Our outerwear accessories were woefully inadequate for Calgary's winters, only because anything designed for warmth was not considered chic. I don't remember any fashionable items like today's tights or tuques. (Whenever I pass the window of a Roots store today, I picture Centralites flocking to its doors. Its fashion style is so "Central.") Lois and I walked to and from school—including the trek home for lunch—every single day, regardless of the weather, and you'd have thought we were paupers by our attire.

"Eleanor, you're not walking to school like that are you?" Mother gasps. It's 15 below, and I'm heading out the door in bare legs, no boots and no gloves, although I do have my wool bandana tied under my chin. "You'll get chilblains going out like that."

"Does your mother threaten you with chilblains?" I ask Lois, as we draw our hands up into our sleeves for protection. "I don't even know what they are, do you?"

"Your mom, too?" she sighs.

The suggestion was that I'd get irrevocable complications from this mystery condition, but the worst I ever got was a gruesome case of deep purple legs dotted with hideous patches of white. (Maybe *that's* chilblains!) On bitterly cold days, the school yielded to us wearing slacks, but we never got away with it for more than one day. If the cold snap persisted, we had to carry a skirt and change in the locker room. On slack days, half

Off to Heintzman's in our Hudson Bays. Me, Lois, Helen. circa 1953

the Central female population wore Black Watch plaid slacks and red Hudson Bay Blanket carcoats. Onlookers must have thought Central had gone to uniforms.

Fads were often introduced by kids who'd accompanied their parents on a Great Falls shopping trip, a popular and trendy thing to do, because at that time, the States had goods unavailable in Canada, prices were considerably lower and our dollar was close to par. My family never did the Great Falls loop, but Lois once brought me back a red Dan River jacket, the rage of the day. It was a plain cotton zippered affair—about as ordinary an item as you could imagine—but somehow it caught on, and you were a nobody if you didn't own a Dan River.

Shoe styles came and went as they do today, and it was costly keeping our feet current. Navy and white saddle oxfords

With Dad – in my Dan River jacket. circa. 1954

were popular until the arrival of white bucks, which took the school by storm. They were made of suede, and came with a little chalk bag for whacking them with as a means of cleaning. Jim was the first in my class to show up with white bucks, and I remember all the guys jokingly circling him at arm's length to avoid scuffing his exclusive footwear. White T-strap shoes gained popularity among the girls about the same time the boys were migrating to brown suede desert boots, both styles having cropped up off and on ever since. But my all time favorite, which has never been replicated, was the Corey shoe; a flat, fairly dressy, navy suede shoe with a choice of two or three different accents. Some had buckles, mine had two small suede tassels on the sides. They were pricey and only available at Robert's Shoes, a high end shop on Eighth Avenue. They were worth every hard earned penny.

One other fashion item we all carried was an Elizabeth Arden kit, not because it was particularly needed or useful, but like the Dan River jacket, it somehow escalated into a must-have fad. It was a flat leather, zippered kit, perhaps 5 inches by 6 inches, outfitted with a brush, comb, mirror, lipstick and sample sized creams of some description. Mine was cream colored and went everywhere with me, although I don't think I used half of its contents.

I wore my hair long in grades ten and eleven, and in the absence of today's invaluable hair dryers, had to twist it into pin curls every night before bed. Then I'd toss all night with the pins poking my scalp. If I inserted them into freshly washed hair, it would still be wet in the morning and I'd have to comb out each section very gingerly in order to salvage the curl. This nightly ritual was nothing short of insanity considering I had naturally curly hair. The thing was, Mother Nature botched the job, not only curling one side up and the other side down, but getting the up side curlier than the down side. Mother Nature made a mess of my cousin's hair, too, except hers was bone straight—just not straight enough. Poor Audrey was forced to lay her head on the ironing board and do the job right. In Grade Twelve the "duck tail" came into vogue, a style perfectly suited to my hair, and I was actually satisfied for a brief moment in time.

There was another intriguing fad worn by a group of guys, quite foreign to us, who lurked about the streets of Calgary—the zoot suit—recognizable by its jacket with super wide shoulders, narrowing to a 'V' at the bottom. The pants, referred to as "drapes," had high, tight, pleated waists, widening to enormous baggy knees, then narrowing again to ankle-hugging cuffs. The outfit's trademark was a long gold chain dangling in a loop down the side of one leg. We never knew who the "Zoot Suiters" were or where they came from, but of one thing we were certain—they did not attend Central High School.

Update:

The Bowness Golf and Country Club burned to the ground in the early morning hours of Sunday March 9, 1997. Arson was suspected.

Central High School closed in 1965 and housed Continuing

Education for a number of years before reopening as the Dr. Carl Safran School serving special needs students. It is now leased to Rundle College, a private school for junior high students. I don't know if its ceiling still leaks. Developers have been knocking on the school's door for some time with offers to purchase the property for apartments, but my old neighborhood, Connaught, is fighting to maintain Central's history as well as its surrounding green space, a precious commodity in the area. Needless to say, I'm cheering for the Connaught team. Central Memorial School opened in 1969 in Southwest Calgary, inheriting all the original school's war memorials, trophies, school colors and team names. I trust it's upholding our proud tradition.

Chapter 9

—JUNIOR PURSUITS—

On a typical day, I'd head to one of my favorite sport venues to find some action, and if that failed to produce, I knew where to look next. My Scarboro gang collected regularly at one of three places: the church on the east, the coulee on the west, or Triangle Park in the middle. We had an uncanny nose for which of the three was the location of the moment.

The Church

Scarboro Avenue United Church was just like home; the doors were never locked, I could come and go at will, and I was loved unconditionally. And just like home, it carried expectations and responsibilities. On one hand, we kids took the church for granted, but on the other, we sensed how privileged we were. The freedom to meet our friends and play unsupervised in this safe haven was a privilege we never abused. We were in seventh heaven when the church added a spacious hall in 1951, outfitting it with badminton and basketball equipment. We looked after our church home, always leaving it the way we found it. I admit there was one day, however, when the janitor might have found a mysterious stream of water running between the basement door and the kitchen sink. Actually, there's a good chance it was closer to a river.

Helen and I were tobogganing on the hill behind the church

and got the bright idea of creating our very own luge track. We located some pails in the church's storage room, filled them with water, then lugged them out to the hill and poured, tramping in and out for the better part of an afternoon. I don't think our project turned out exactly as we envisioned, but we convinced ourselves that our toboggans—fashioned from cardboard boxes— were ripping down that hill much faster than before.

Two midweek favorites at the church were Explorers and later C.G.I.T.—Canadian Girls in Training. We were never taxied to activities, regardless of distance or weather, but never felt deprived

CGIT camp.
Margaret, Elaine, Margaret, Mary. circa. 1951

since we considered the to and from to be the highlight of any event. I loved Tuesday nights when I'd meet my gang on the corner, and we'd head down to the church in a pack, stretching the ten minute walk into a half hour, attend our C.G.I.T. festivities, then kill an hour and a half dawdling back to the corner, where we'd loiter some more before calling it a night. We were completely oblivious to the dark, the cold, or the time. Mother trusted my gang implicitly, but Don labeled us the Craziest Girls In Town, and still laughably claims the neighborhood was terrorized every Tuesday night.

One person who might have agreed with Don, was our C.G.I.T. leader, Marilyn Perkins. "Perky," just five years older than us girls, was blazing an impossible trail for us to follow, serving her church and community with staggering energy and dedication. We decided we must be God's chosen sent to test her. It's a testament to her moral fiber that she not only withstood the weekly abuse we dished out at C.G.I.T., but willingly submitted herself to further punishment by funneling us into one of her celebrated choirs.

"I wonder how smart she is," I think to myself at the very first practice, while cleverly mouthing the words without uttering a sound. Tucked way back here in the back row, I figure, *"She'll never know the difference."*

Without skipping a beat, she raises her eyebrows in my direction, and mouths —audibly— "Eleanor, sing!"

Marilyn enriched the lives of countless thousands through her extraordinary musical gifts and daily acts of kindness. We rose up in anger the day she received a disheartening diagnosis of cancer that steadily took her down, but not without a feisty, Marilyn-style fight. I can see her shaking her finger at God, "But I've still got miles to go before I sleep." At her memorial service, I encountered Mary, a beloved C.G.I.T. mate, and we smugly agreed that we had played a critical role in the development of one of Perky's defining attributes—fortitude. I also wondered if my mouthing episode wasn't the initial inspiration for one of her notable witticisms, "If you're going to fake it, move your lips faster."

The church also meant Sunday mornings for my family, without fail, and properly attired. The men of the household wore suits and ties, and the women wore dresses that modestly covered the shoulders, even in summer. And hats. Compulsory, ill-fitting, cursed hats.

"I hate this hat. It's too small and it makes me look dumb." Every hat in the city of Calgary was too small for my big head.

"You look lovely in that hat. The blue is so nice with your eyes."

"I don't care if it matches my eyes, it doesn't fit. Why do I have to wear a hat, anyway?"

"Now dear, you know you have to wear a hat." I never won the battle of the hat.

Our minister, Dr. Sam Parsons, was a giant of a man in every way—body, mind and spirit—and we adored him. His repertoire and delivery of children's stories was almost as good as my dad's, and almost worth the insufferable hat. His sermons were masterpieces,too, although on occasion, Dad would suggest a sermon went on too long. "Sam preached a wonderful sermon today," he'd declare, "but he missed a couple of good stopping off places."

Dr. Parsons had another lure in the form of postcard-sized attendance cards, designed in bright colors with little squares running around the perimeter, one for every Sunday of the year. Standing at the front of the sanctuary, he'd punch the appropriate square of each kid's card like a train conductor, as we exited single file mid way through the service. "Good for you, Eleanor, you haven't missed a Sunday," he'd beam. "See you next week." The cards served the dual purpose of aiding Dr. Parsons with the names of his little lambs, while challenging them to perfect attendance.

Our family habitually sat in the same pew, a common custom among regular attendees, who seemed to claim squatter's rights. The Kings sat five pews from the front, left side, middle aisle, parents book-ending the children. Mother loved singing hymns and must have been grateful that we separated her from the distraction of Dad's enthusiastic, though monotone delivery.

Needless to say, much of the congregation sat behind us, although the Littles were in front and to the right, and the Edwards were directly across from us. *"Lucky Marj,"* I'd think with envy, *"her family gets the pew with the hearing device because Grandpa Patterson can't hear. Sure wish I could try listening through one of those things. Lucky Marj, she has a grandpa."*

The Nelson family sat off to the left of us, their widowed mother wedged between her brood to maintain order. *"Lucky Mary, her hat looks so nice on her. No wonder—it fits."*

"It's rude to stare," Mother would tug at my sleeve as I craned over my shoulder to find Aunt Lil. *"Where is she today?"* I'd wonder, if she wasn't in her designated pew behind us, certain, however, that she'd be performing some very necessary duty like filling the communion glasses. *"How does she fill those miniscule glasses without spilling grape juice all over the tray?"* Then Don would tug my other sleeve, and point out Mrs. Robison's solo listed in the service bulletin, or a duet by Marilyn Featherston and Diane Woodcock, and my heart would sing. I loved my Scarboro Church family.

The Coulee

As young kids, the coulee west of Scarboro was a playground for all seasons—skating, skiing and tobogganing in winter, and just knocking about in summer. A natural spring trickled through its base, producing a mile long skating rink when frozen, and a race course for popsicle sticks during spring thaw. The coulee was also home to a variety of flowers and wildlife, and during popsicle derby season, I'd watch daily for the velvety, purple-headed crocuses to make their first appearance. I was terrified—and incensed—the day Janice and I were innocently combing the brush in search of our first crocus, and a cranky weasel charged out of nowhere and bit her on the hand. So much for all those adult assurances that an unprovoked animal won't attack. Why didn't someone tell the weasel that?

John's dog Rags was another matter. Rags regularly provoked the resident porcupine, and would arise from the coulee with a snout full of quills, yelping his head off. He'd endure an agonizing extraction by John and his buddy, Johnny, then doggedly return for another dose. When it became abundantly apparent that Rags did not possess a shred of common sense, the boys one day decided to take matters into their own hands.

"I'm not pulling quills out of your dumb dog one more time," complains Johnny. "We've gotta get the porcupine. It's the only answer."

"How d'ya figure on doin' that?" replies John, drawn, however, to a possible solution to his prickly problem.

"Easy, we'll capture him in a box and haul him out of the coulee."

They straight-away recruit Ritchie and Mike, and gather the necessary equipment: a broom, a large box with a wire grid at one end, a matching sized piece of plywood and a wagon. Then the Scarboro mafia descends into the coulee.

After a brief time lying in wait, their prey blows his cover, and Mike approaches cautiously, using the broom to coax him toward the awaiting box. When Mike gets the porcupine within striking range, the others pounce, flipping the box over their victim. They slide the plywood underneath, hoist the works onto the wagon and emerge from the coulee triumphant.

The boys strut their stuff around their quarry, gloating over their accomplishment—until Johnny, suddenly looking very perplexed, cries halt to their victory dance. "What do we do with him now?" he asks the bragging braves. In their infinite wisdom, no one has considered anything beyond getting this critter into a box.

"I know," says John, in a flash of brilliance, "let's put him on display and charge the neighborhood kids five cents to view him." John's suggestion is met with instant approval.

"We can entice them with a free souvenir quill," adds Johnny, as the budding entrepreneurs quickly establish the ground work that will pave the way to riches.

"We need to advertise," says Mike, the business head of the group. "We've got to spread the word. We'll make posters and deliver them to every house."

By now, however, night is falling, and a more pressing issue confronts them—the porcupine's overnight requirements. Ritchie readily volunteers his backyard, so the weary tribe wheels Porky to his sleeping quarters and tucks him in for the night, with food, water and a blanket. They will get an early start the next day, and the neighborhood kids will flock to see their amazing, live exhibit.

Ritchie spends a fitful night tossing and turning with excitement, and at daybreak, he can't wait a minute longer to check on Porky. Dashing out in pajamas and bare feet, he breathlessly lifts the blanket, and there, staring back at him—is an empty box! He races desperately about the yard, checking behind every bush. "Here Porky! Here Porky! Po-o-o-r-r-r-ke-e!" He clambers over the back fence and down the hill behind, beating through the brush in a frantic search for the escapee. Porky is gone!

Meanwhile, Mike is yawning at his breakfast table. His mother—like all mafia mothers—is not privy to the previous day's activities. She greets him with some entertaining, wake-up news.

*Ritchie, Rags, Bobby.
circa. 1948*

"I just heard a funny story on the radio," she exclaims. "Some man phoned the station to report a curious sight. Apparently, on his way to work this morning, he saw a porcupine ambling across Twelfth Avenue—right below your friend Ritchie's house. I wonder how in the world that creature got there?"

One of my regrettably few memories of Uncle Harry was playing war in the coulee trenches, a training field used by Currie Barracks. I can't remember what we used for guns, but Uncle Harry always managed to scrounge at least one piece of wearing apparel for each of us—a jacket, belt, helmet, or his *pièce de résistance*, an authentic W.W.I gas mask. We'd drag ourselves along the ground by our elbows guerrilla style, slither into opposing trenches, then slowly surface as we'd seen soldiers do in the movies. When a head appeared above a trench, the enemy FIRED—then real life fighting began as we argued over who fired first, who hit their intended target, and who was supposed to be dead. Uncle Harry was a master at talking one of the troops into surrendering with a white flag or convincing both to sign a peace treaty. The diplomatic corps would have hired him in a minute.

One other activity in that neck of the woods was horseback riding, something I would never have done without a push from my pal Lois. We started out renting Shetland ponies from Ovans's Stables, a block or so west of Currie Barracks. The ponies were ornery little critters that I'd spend nine tenths of my rental time coaxing from the corral, my legs spread-eagled uselessly above their bulging girth. I couldn't believe my good fortune the day one stubborn pony quite unexpectedly capitulated to our battle of wills by plodding out onto the prairie grass with seemingly full cooperation. Then with even less warning—and long before my time was up—it not only spun for home, but impudently scraped me off against a telephone pole conveniently planted at the final turn. I never went back to Ovans's.

It was time to graduate to the full-sized horses at Currie Barracks anyway, where the quality of the mounts and my confidence level improved only marginally. Somehow I managed to develop a rapport with a horse named Strawberry, a gentle, understanding mare that I occasionally rode all the way through the coulee and right down Scarboro Avenue to show my mother, and anyone else interested. Strawberry was very tall and I was very short, so I had to tie her to the back porch, which provided the necessary platform for remounting. But even Strawberry didn't get me beyond being a white knuckled equestrian, and to this day I harbor resentment over all the repetitive, idiotic coaching I received to, "show 'er who's boss." As if I didn't know!

Jean and Strawberry on Scarboro Avenue. circa. 1951

Ice Skating

The coulee also launched my skating career. When conditions were just right, I could stand below Seventeenth Avenue at the upper end of its frozen spring, point my skates north, spread open my gray flared coat, and let the wind sweep me all the way down to Twelfth Avenue. Then I'd button my coat against the headwind, dig in the toe picks of my impossibly dull skates and fight my way back to the starting position, where I'd turn around, spread my wings and sail again, repeating the loop until I dropped.

The natural rink was augmented with a community rink, economically flooded inside the confines of the summer tennis courts. This is where I actually took my first strides. My friends Helen and Jean patiently propped me up, while I resolutely wobbled round and round the rink partly on my blades, mostly on the side of my boots. Small wonder my skates were dull. But from the first tentative steps, I knew skating was for me, and forever after, I equated lacing up with pure joy. To this day, nothing carries me back to my childhood like a pair of skates.

When I was still little, Ole, the rink caretaker, laced my skates for me, and only Ole had the knack for getting them just right. On Saturdays, I'd spend the entire day at the rink and when temperatures plummeted I was in and out of the clubhouse repeatedly to remove my skates and warm my feet on the pot belly stove. Once I could feel my toes again, I pulled my skates back on and Ole cheerfully tightened them up without complaint. No matter how many times the ritual was repeated, he never complained. I've never forgotten that dear, kind man and his role in launching my lifelong love affair with skating.

One of my happiest visions of the rink below is that of Mother and Dad skating together—a lost art. I see Dad with his right arm hooked under Mother's left, propelling her anti-clockwise around the rink to the sound of *The Skater's Waltz* or *Syncopated Clock* crackling from the loud speakers, their blades scraping perilously close, but miraculously never tangling. Mother's tiny little feet appear so much longer in her speed skates. I remember Uncle Harry and Aunt Lil being there, too, but I see Aunt Lil propelling herself around the ice, because Uncle Harry is playing British Bulldog and Pom Pom Pull-Away with us kids. "Pom pom pull-away, if you don't come, I'll pull you away."

At some point in the late forties, the community rink was moved from its wind-sheltered hideaway in the coulee up to the area behind Sunalta School. The joy of skating continued, but the new setting never had the ambiance of the old.

In Junior High, the rink became a stage for one of our first romantic rituals in a setting far less intimidating than a dance floor. The rink ceremony was an embarrassingly stupid game of chase, but it had complex guidelines. The game required one compulsory piece of attire for the girls—a bandana—or large square scarf folded cornerwise into a triangle, tied under the chin. (I notice the Queen has clung to this fashion accessory all these years. She's still photographed wearing one when she's out walking her Corgis behind the Palace.) Once the girls began circling the ice with their bandanas in place, the game was underway.

The boys would slowly trickle onto the ice, casually circling both the rink and the girls while feigning minimal interest. Then, when you least expected, one would silently glide up behind you and snap your bandana, a signal for you to commence your racing speed which justified him giving chase. If he caught up to you and successfully plucked your bandana from your head—guaranteed if you played your cards right—then you got to chase him the rest of the day to try and get it back. The game's success depended largely on how effectively the girl tied her bandana—too tight put the kibosh on the earnest suitor successfully removing it, but ridiculously loose was shamefully obvious. You knew it was just right if he could get it off, but your head was jerked in the process. One other consideration for the girl was her skating speed. If she was an exceptional skater, she risked eliminating certain guys from the chase, but, as with the bandana, ridiculously slow— shamefully obvious. Stage management was extremely complicated; you had to skate at a just-catchable speed wearing a just-snappable bandana. We got very good at it.

By high school, the dance of the bandana was *passé*. On

Sunday afternoons we headed for the shoddy old Victoria Arena where the big time action was—*sans* bandanas. The arena exposed us to a larger circle of guys who were much too sophisticated for the chase and snatch routine. It was their custom to glide up beside you and simply invite you for a skate, as if it were a dance. A real coup was an invitation from one of the "rink rats," young hockey players who earned pin money and skate time on the rink maintenance crew. They were strong skaters and could sweep you around the ice at twice the speed you could ever achieve under your own steam. A rink rat's arm was also a great asset for maintaining your balance among the jostling throngs, something you were especially grateful for late in the day when the friction from all the blades had turned the ice into a swimming pool, and a single fall spelled disaster. My favorite rink rat was Ron "Squeak" Leopold who so effortlessly propelled me to Barbara Ann Scott heights.

The climax of every outing at the Arena was a visit to Pete's Popcorn Stand, a colorful little free-standing shop parked on the northwest corner of Seventeenth Avenue and Macleod Trail, a prime location for capturing the Arena and Stampede trade. Its carnival-like decor and heavenly aroma hovering in the air made it impossible to pass. Pete produced popcorn that's never been equaled. A copper pot that resembled a watering can rested on a warmer behind his popcorn machine, and through its long, thin spout he poured copious amounts of hot melted butter—*real* butter—into our bags. Only at Pete's did the popcorn at the bottom of the bag get as thoroughly coated as the popcorn at the top.

The Stampede Corral opened to great accolades in 1950 and, although we considered it fabulous beyond measure, it was like the Scarboro rink moving to the top of the hill—our sentimental attachments forever remained with our first love.

Roller Skating

Roller skating was summer's poor substitute for ice skating, a fact the boys apparently recognized, because it was an activity undertaken almost  exclusively by girls. Our all-metal skates attached to the soles of our shoes, and had to be adjusted for length and width with a specific key. My skates chronically fell off, so I carried my key on a string around my neck where it was readily available for readjustments. The wheels vibrated like mad on the sidewalks and clunk, clunk, clunked rhythmically as you rolled over the cracks. The skates had no braking mechanism, so the only way to stop was to roll onto the boulevard, an extremely dangerous exercise at high speed. The only protective equipment I ever wore was on my knees. I wore large, thick scabs.

One of the most terrifying experiences of my life took place on my roller skates, the day I challenged the Sunalta bus to a race down the Scarboro hill, too dim-witted to recognize the danger it posed. The bus, uninformed of the challenge of course, jumped to an early lead through the first fifty-yard slope leading to a near ninety degree turn, but I was gathering so much speed I suddenly realized, *"I can't possibly make the turn at this clip!"* Yet I did— somehow—teetering precariously on the edges of my outer wheels. But there was no celebrating, because I was now freewheeling past the bus down the long, steep hill at breakneck speed, each crack in the sidewalk coming faster than the last. My legs were humming from the vibration of my skates, then numbing with fear as the bottom of the hill loomed, and I faced the impossible assignment of the next turn, at triple the speed of the last one.

Aware that catching a wheel on the boulevard would send me cartwheeling to instant death, I locked myself into a tuck and focused on maintaining all eight wheels in contact with the cement. With every approaching inch, I thanked God for the city engineer who'd carved the turn onto Twelfth Avenue in a wide, sweeping arc, giving me a remote chance. But I wasn't kidding myself, it still called for a guardian angel. I don't remember seeing her—or anything else—through that turn, but I know she was there, and waving her wand like she'd never waved it before. It's my only explanation for how I executed that turn. I could not believe that I was actually coasting along Twelfth Avenue—alive. Not only that, a quick shoulder check revealed I had beaten the bus!

Swimming

Calgary had two public swimming pools in my youth, the Municipal, an outdoor pool just north of the armories on Eleventh Street and the indoor Crystal nearby on the northeast corner of Fourth Avenue and Tenth Street. I was only allowed in one of the pools.

"Aw, gee, Mom," I pester, "the other kids get to go to the Crystal."

"Maybe so, dear, but I just don't think it's very clean."

"But its got a great big, jungle style rope for swinging into the pool. The Municipal hasn't got a rope." But Mother, ever mindful of the threat of polio, holds firm with her conviction, and I never get to play Jane.

I understand I also missed the seductive torso of the Crystal's famous lifeguard, Walter Petrigo, who eventually became an esteemed Calgary Herald photographer. In spite of being denied those two attractions, I spent many contented summer days at the Municipal.

The Municipal had morning and afternoon swims, and the pool and locker rooms were entirely cleared in between. Helen and Jean, my swimming companions, not only preferred the less populated morning time, but aimed for front of the line at its 8:00 a.m. opening to get their money's worth. Being a nocturnal animal, the very thought of rising at that hour was abhorrent, especially when I didn't have to, but the number of times I did it is testament to how much I loved swimming. Also, the reward of being first one in went a long way to ease the pain.

Mother never enrolled me in swimming lessons, so I became adept at eavesdropping on group lessons from a discreet distance, then practicing the instructions on my own after the class had dispersed. I backed up my pool work with breathing exercises every night in the bathtub at home. I remember the lifeguard making us swim two widths of the pool before allowing us into the deep end, and I was extremely pleased with myself when I passed his test before most graduates of the class.

Now and then Bill Patrick, one of Canada's premier international divers—the Municipal's answer to Walter Petrigo—arrived at the pool to practice, and the screaming, splashing sounds fell silent as all heads turned to watch. But casual watching wasn't enough for me. I'd sit poolside for as long as Bill was performing, studying every twist and turn of his body, quite confident I could learn to dive by remote just as I'd learned to swim. I got as far as a running dive off the low board, which would have earned a '2' at best for style.

One other lasting memory of the pools was the frightening summers in the early fifties, when the city closed them down due to polio epidemics. Schools and theaters were also closed during severe outbreaks. My fear of the disease grew to terror when three children of a neighboring family were struck down, one condemned to a wheelchair for the rest of her days. How relieved we were when the miraculous Salk vaccine ended the scourge almost overnight.

Tennis

The Calgary Tennis Club originally shared the coulee with the skating rink, but by the time I picked up a racquet, it had moved to its current location at the foot of the hill below Scarboro Church. It upheld the All England tradition of a rigid all white dress code, although our shoes and socks were usually orange from the shale court surface. Etiquette was the first rule of the day, and the first thing we juniors learned before the Club turned us loose with our racquets. Uncle Harry was a dominant force at the Club in his day, but to my regret, I lost him before reaping the benefit of his willing expertise. He lived long enough, however, to launch his daughter Marion, who carried the King banner to top competitive levels. Old tennis photos of Uncle Harry display a dapper dandy in long white flannel pants—doubtlessly sweltering, but a picture of cool. Shorts were an unthinkable option.

I had a list of reasons as long as my racquet for never progressing beyond the hacker level, everything from not having a single friend interested in playing the game, to my seriously inferior equipment. Dad had a penchant for making do with things second hand, so I was assigned his old wooden Bentley. He did get it restrung once—with catgut—when he discovered I'd been thwacking away on broken strings the entire season. There's no telling how long one set of balls lasted me, but bald and flat didn't really matter considering the state of my racquet. When they lost their bounce entirely, I'd park myself beside the seniors' courts, and eventually someone would grant me their used balls. Alms to the poor. Balls, of course, came in white only.

In spite of everything, I developed a great love for the game, and when I couldn't find anyone to play with, I was perfectly content to curl up behind Marj Eustace's court and watch in awe as she mercilessly ran one more opponent from side to side and back again. Marj was like playing a backboard—*everything* came back—but there was more to her than skill.

"Isn't she the most gorgeous thing on earth," I'd sigh with envy, as my eyes followed her about the court, fairly floating in her trademark one-piece dress with attached undershorts. *"It's not fair for one person to have beauty, charm, grace and talent. Personally, I'd settle for just one of those attributes."* Then I'd catch sight of the frazzled soul on the receiving end of Marj's relentless racquet, and I'd ease back onto my haunches, content with my lot—safe from a demoralizing drubbing behind the fence.

Croquet

The family's signature game was croquet, and our back yard would regularly be found impaled with croquet hoops, ingeniously set at distances and angles to maximize the degree of difficulty. To this day I'm not certain of the conventional layout of a croquet court or the precise rules of play because I have never been exposed to the game outside my own family. We simply yielded to Dad's interpretation of the rules without question, and

Me, minding my own business

I wouldn't entertain playing it any other way. He did invent one rule, though, in an effort to protect the plants from the damage of flying balls. The rule was, if your ball rolled into a flower bed, you were penalized a turn, but since smashing balls to kingdom come was half the fun, we figured it was worth sacrificing a turn, so the plundering of the petunias continued unabated.

The game of croquet can be approached in two ways: you can mind your own business and quietly work your way through the hoops to the finishing peg, or you can sacrifice your own progress to destroy the advancement of the opposition. Everyone hates the guy who employs the latter strategy. We had a neighbor, Rick—the castle door guard Rick— who was a master at it, taking fiendish delight in screaming about the yard smacking any ball he perceived to be in an advantageous position. He was brilliant at it, and retaliation was hopeless because winning for him was incidental, and you certainly couldn't beat him at his game of seek and destroy. Dad, on the other hand, played only to win, and you'd hear an audible moan whenever Rick poked his head around the garage, asking, "Can I play?"

We had another neighbor, Bill, who was a "toe-master." Even after Rick-the-spoiler ruined Bill's ball position, he'd be miraculously perfectly lined up when his next turn rolled around. We finally caught on to his tactic of nudging his ball into position with his toe, but politely ignored it because he never won anyway, and it gave us a laugh.

Mother never played croquet, so the other four of us often became embroiled in an intense doubles challenge. Strategy is of the essence in doubles, so endless time was taken up pouring over every possible alternative for every last shot. Needless to say, after a fifteen minute debate we'd finally settle on a strategy—then miss the shot.

Stan, the destroyer

It wasn't unusual for an after-dinner game to stretch past dark, and Dad would have to angle the car in the driveway so we could finish by headlight.

Triangle Park—Jump-Off for Hijinks

On summer evenings, Triangle Park was *the* place to be. The park had been designed in 1937 as a Coronation project and was the only one of any size in our neighborhood sprinkled with mini decorative parks. Being centrally located, we'd converge on it from every direction, ready for the night's action. We often played touch football until dark, then launched into a game of "seek and go hide," our innovative reversal of its more traditional counterpart. Using the thick patch of bushes in the center of the park, one person hid, and the rest were seekers, stealing silently through the bushes until they found the hider, joining him in his burrow. It was pretty eerie when you suddenly discovered you were the sole remaining seeker, all alone in the pitch dark.

With surprising regularity, a Triangle Park evening evolved into mischief, but clever, creative mischief if I say so myself. Sometimes bordering on brilliant. The old standby was "white rabbit"—ring and run—familiar to every kid since the beginning of time. But Shelbourne Street's gentle curve around one side of the park provided the perfect setting for our exclusive version of the game, which involved a synchronized attack on multiple houses. We'd each select a house, then stand with fingers poised until our appointed captain signaled from one end of the block, and we'd all ring at once. Then we'd dash for the park and dive into the bushes, suppressing giggles at the sight of homeowners peering sheepishly up and down the street at their mystified neighbors doing the same.

We were more selective with our single raids, targeting homes we considered deserving for one lame reason or another. One regular victim spotted us assembling one evening and crouched in readiness when he saw our elected delinquent approaching. A split second after Mike's finger hit the bell, he was dangling by the scruff of his neck, in the fierce grip of his chafing apprehender.

We froze in horror from our hiding places across the street, wondering how Mike was ever going to extricate himself from this alarming predicament. Then, with aplomb beyond belief, he calmly looked his captor in the eye and said, "Good evening sir. Do you happen to know where the King family lives?" Tripping over a profusion of apologies, our mortified neighbor accompanied the polite—and bewildered—young man to the front walk, where, over further apology, he pointed out the King residence down the street. That night we unanimously voted to scratch that neighbor from our hit list.

Wherever there are kids and crabapples, snitching is

inevitable, and Scarboro was a haven for this activity. Two of the best trees in the neighborhood grew in my own back yard, but openly picking is no substitute for snitching, so we roamed the alleys sampling everyone else's orchard. It didn't take us long to zero in on the biggest and sweetest crop in town, and within days we'd beaten an access tunnel through the hedge protecting it. One dark evening, the owner crept onto his chaise lounge, where he remained in silent stillness ready to pounce, just as our white rabbit neighbor had done previously.

One by one we crawled through the rabbit sized hole, while the conspirator resisted attack until every last one of us was in his lair. Then he lunged! Eight shrieking kids trying to scramble through one small hole must have been a sight to behold. I only know I was the second of only two to escape, and I ran down that alley faster than I knew how. I never looked back. Word has it subsequent generations have discovered our famous crabapple tree and the raids continue. My informant offered no information on the cunning of the new homeowner.

Two of our most wicked stunts were one-time affairs—the infamous bus blockade and the house-of-grass caper. Tiny Watson, our one-of-a-kind, eternally good-natured Sunalta bus driver was everyone's favorite. Tiny had a habit of surveying the streets for stragglers, and was known to wait for a commuter spotted half a block away, following which he'd simply adjust his speed the required amount to maintain his schedule. I couldn't believe my eyes the day he parked at our corner stop with doors ajar, calmly waiting for a woman tottering down the street in her spike heeled shoes. Gasping for breath, she stumbled on the bottom step of the bus and snapped a heel off cleanly, collapsing in despair over her dilemma. Tiny nonchalantly picked her up, dusted her off, and sent her scurrying back home for a change of shoes, while he waited. The ride downtown that day was an autobahn experience.

Because Tiny was so adept at accommodating delays, he was able to work in a late evening cigarette break at the end of the route on Sunderland Avenue, where the bus was almost always empty. He would enjoy a leisurely interlude, then put the pedal to the metal and still make it downtown in the allotted time. One night, when my gang was wandering aimlessly through Triangle Park, we spotted Tiny, and someone recognized the potential his evening habit presented.

"Hurry up, guys. If we get started right away, we'll be ready for him before he returns on his last run." We disperse up the alley adjacent to the bus stop, scouring for boulders.

"Margaret, that one's not big enough."

"But I can't carry one any bigger."

"Just roll it on the ground then. They've gotta be really big."

Grunting and groaning, we lug and roll an impressive pile of ammunition to our stronghold behind a border of thick fur trees lining the property of the residence beside the smoke/bus stop. Then we crouch in waiting.

"Are you sure Tiny will stop for a break this time? What if he's too late?"

"You don't know Tiny. He always figures out a way to take a break."

"Sh-h-h, here he comes!"

Tiny arrives right on schedule, and as usual, there isn't a single passenger getting on or off the bus.

"We're in luck," a breathless voice gasps in the dark, as we watch Tiny plant his feet on the dash, tip back his cap, and light up.

"Now!" our commander orders, as Tiny inhales his first moment of ecstasy. The juvenile marauders silently and swiftly roll out their ammo and block his back wheels. Delaying to the last possible moment, Tiny guns the motor . . . br-r-m . . . br-r-m-m . . . **br-r-r-m-m.**

"What the #*?&*?@+#>!!???"

I guarantee Tiny did not make schedule that night. The cigarette breaks continued, but never again with the same repose. From that night on, Tiny did his puffing *outside* the bus, leaning vigilantly against the back wheels.

I have no idea who initiated the house-of-grass caper, but I'm inexplicably tempted to point my finger at Cousin Ritchie—which he will inevitably deny. In any event, I reluctantly confess to being a willing participant, and can only defend our actions on the certainty that the devil inhabited our very souls that night.

In summer, the unattended grass in Sunalta's schoolyard became long and dry, eventually requiring a city crew to knock it down, leaving behind our villainous field of schemes. Across from the schoolyard, a house with a small enclosed front porch beckoned irresistibly. At nightfall we assembled two groups; one to scoop up armloads of grass from the schoolyard and toss it over the fence, and the other to transport it across the street and pack it into the porch—clear up to its peaked roof. It was a work of art. Next, a volunteer knocker bearing a long stick, poked it through the thatch, rapped on the door, and we ran—so far and so fast we missed the entire resulting drama. I tossed in bed all that night, but was it due to guilt or was I was just ticked with myself for crafting a brilliant scheme, laboring to accomplish it, then running scared and missing the thrill of the intended climax— seeing the homeowner shrouded in hay?

For a period, my flock of felons had an overpowering fascination with invading sites where we had no business being. The mission was never to break and enter, steal or vandalize, but merely to enter for the thrill of spooking about in unfamiliar territory in the dark. Most of our hijinks were relatively risk free, but a few brought unexpected danger.

Two outside jobs that gave me a good scare took place at industries down on Tenth Avenue below Scarboro—Cushing Mills and Calgary Concrete. I snuck into Cushing's lumber yard with my friend Elaine one afternoon, and was immediately drawn to a huge pyramid of sawdust, which looked for all the world like an oversized sand box.

"C'mon," I urge Elaine, "let's climb it." I enter the heap of sawdust, brainlessly assuming I'll be able to crawl on its surface, but I quickly discover I'm sinking up to my haunches with every step.

"I'm not going in there," says Elaine, sensing impending danger. "You're getting in awful deep," she warns. "You'd better get out while you can."

Just then an unfamiliar whirring sound erupts above, and I look up just in time to see a fresh supply of sawdust raining upon me from a giant overhead pipe. In seconds I'm buried alive and frantically gasping for air. With each consecutive breath, I inhale more sawdust, a sensation that defies description. Instinctively, I flail my arms and legs in a desperate struggle to keep my head "above water," and miraculously, discover myself actually "swimming" my way to safety. I flop, gasping and panting, before my friend, who by this time is holding her sides laughing at the ridiculous sight of the sputtering, sawdust-coated rag doll at her feet.

"Some friend you are," I fume, "I could have choked to death and you would have just stood there and laughed. It's not funny, you know." Wheezing and shaking, I stomp home to face the tedious task of picking sawdust from all my two thousand body parts. It surfaced for days.

Calgary Concrete, which we kids referred to as the "cement factory," was down the street west of the lumber yard. It had an enormous conveyor belt running from the ground to a height probably the equivalent of three stories high. I had a strong aversion to heights, but egged on by my pack one aimless night, I couldn't refuse their challenge to scale it to the top. I kept very focused for close to four fifths of the way up, carefully observing my own mandate, *"Don't look down,"* as I crept steadily upward on my hands and knees. Then suddenly I froze. But it wasn't the height psyching me, it was the demons of the lumber yard returning to haunt me. The belt beneath me was going to mobilize just as surely as that tube of sawdust had, and nothing was going to convince me otherwise. Not even the fact that it was pitch dark, after hours and nary a worker or watchman was on the premises. That belt was a millisecond away from rolling—rumbling me to the top and dropping me like a stone through sixty feet of vacuum into a gooey pool of sludge below! Then I'd sink to my death . . . glug, glug, glug. There'd be no swimming out of this.

The rumbling indeed began, but it was my body shaking in terror. The backward descent was interminable, hand and knee an inch at a time, too panic stricken to maneuver onto one of the support ladders or even rotate and skid forward in a crouch. With every inch I begged the belt for mercy, *"Don't start now, don't start now,"* repeating the order non-stop until I dropped off the bottom in a quivering heap. Not until I found my legs did I discover the blood oozing from my hands and knees, solidly embedded with gravel chips. I never again stepped foot on the cement works or lumber yard properties. I moved directly to inside jobs, like the "vinegar works" further west down the street.

Climbing into Western Vinegars was a classic example of doing something just because it was there. It was also the last unchallenged target on Tenth Avenue. In those days the police had established an inventive protocol for dealing with intruders such as us, whom they correctly determined to be nothing more than nuisances. Wearing their most convincing gruff cop demeanor, they'd line us up and ceremoniously record everyone's name in their little black book. I assume the formality was designed to appease adult complainants while worrying us kids—now officially on record—into behaving, at least for the rest of the week. I expect our *records* hit a waste basket at the end of every shift.

As it happened, someone blew the whistle on us the night we invaded the "vinegar works," and one by one we crawled back out of our entry window into the arms of the law. Trembling in fear, we each identified ourselves for the record book. The last to give her name was a friend whose last name was Lemon, and the burliest cop glared at her and growled, "Aha, that explains it! We've been getting a lot of complaints lately from people tasting lemon in their vinegar!" Only when we detected a grin spreading across his face did we laugh with relief.

On another occasion, the King cousins entered the record books for playing touch football in a park designated for walkers only. One by one, we dutifully recited our names: Frank King, Eleanor King, Richard King . . . until there was one left. "Donald King," my brother announced defiantly, to which Cousin Art quickly shook his head and cautioned, "You should tell 'em your right name, George." I thought Don was going to faint dead away. The cops, who didn't care if he was Don or George or Harry, had trouble suppressing grins as they mumbled, "any more Kings around here?" before heading off to strike fear in the hearts of some more innocent kids. Art was laughing so hard he could barely breathe.

The inside job at Fourex Bakery on Eleventh Street West was a piece of cake. We always passed Fourex on our way to and from the swimming pool, a habit that produced a curious mingling of smells that is still imprinted on my brain—the soft aroma of fresh bread wafting through the air and the pungent odor of chlorine clinging to my hair. But Fourex had another attraction that held our attention—a huge wrought iron flour chute equipped with a heavy flip-up lid that didn't appear to have a lock on it. One night our curiosity drove us to test it, and we discovered that indeed it was not secured. But it was impossibly heavy.

"Okay, guys, all together, h-e-a-v-e!" Slowly, the monstrous weight rises.

"You guys hold it, and I'll get in the chute," I offer, scrambling inside and sliding to never never land with visions of sugar plums dancing in my head. Clunk! My exhausted accomplices drop the lid.

"Visions, my foot. I'm blind as a bat down here. Black-outs were never this dark." My heart races as I grope about, hoping at least my nose will lead me to the veritable treasure trove of goodies that my mind's eye sees about me. I grow madder by the minute, as I run my hands across one table after another without landing on a single delicacy. Then my conscience gets in on the act.

"What'll you do if you find a cookie?" asks that still small voice, challenging me to the eighth commandment.

"Eat it, of course," I snap, *"what's one cookie out of mountains, eaten right on the premises. That's not stealing, is it? . . . Is it?"*

But I don't wrestle with the moral dilemma for long, because the spookiness of the place is getting to me, and I head directly for the chute. The chute? *"Where is the blinkin' chute?"* I panic, fumbling in circles, tripping on flour sacks and knocking off rolling pins. I finally find it, only to discover, to my horror, that a chute dusted with flour is nearly impossible to negotiate *up*hill. What to do?

I remove my shoes and socks, stuff them in my shirt, and

spread eagled—with sticky feet—paw my way up the sides of the chute to the lid. For a brief moment, I envision the unthinkable—my friends have gone home and I'm trapped for the night. One rap brings instant relief, as the lid creaks open to a chorus of grunts and groans. The Pillsbury dough girl is sprung from her misadventure—without so much as a donut for her daring.

I wouldn't swear to it, but the Fourex incident might have taken place on the way home from our botched Municipal Pool invasion, probably in an effort to salvage our bruised egos. The Municipal was always packed, and I used to dream of just once having it all to myself. One night a few of us decided to make it a reality.

After the pool closed we scaled the fence, slithered into the water, and with self-satisfied smirks, glided about in silence, lapping up our private piece of heaven. Then it dawned on us that silence in a pool was not our idea of heaven. Never imagining there'd be a watchman on the premises, we threw caution to the wind, and set about our customary shenanigans of splashing, dunking and belly flopping. The watchman had evidently fallen asleep, and with any self control, we might have escaped detection indefinitely. But our skullduggery wakened him, and he ushered us out forthwith, our tails between our legs. We kicked ourselves all the way home. We suspected he continued to nod on the job the rest of the summer, but we never mustered the courage to put our conjecture to the test.

On rare occasions a new house would be constructed in Scarboro, the result of a homeowner with a double lot electing to sell one. We'd immediately claim the property as our after-dark playground, using the excavation for leaping contests, and the framework as a jungle gym for general monkey shines. The highlight of these evenings was the arrival of our cycling commissionaire making his rounds.

"Here he comes," our spotter signals, and we take up our posts. Still as mice, we wait until he is right in front of the house—then leap—devilishly popping in and out of every window frame in the place like *Laugh-In* characters.

"Hey Commish, up here."

"Commish, over this way."

"I'm down here, Commish."

He shakes his flashlight threateningly, and vows to catch and punish every one of us, but we're brazenly confident he isn't about to risk life or limb giving chase over terrain where our skill and spunk provide a distinct advantage.

The commisionaire may well have spared himself a broken leg by wisely not pursuing the pop-up pests. It was always a sad day when a contractor secured the doors and windows of our adopted playhouse, locking out all our fun.

Island Parks

As little kids, visiting any playground or park was cause for excitement, but a day at one of the two river islands—St. George's Island or Bowness Park—was an event. Each held inviting attractions, but St. George's Island, with its zoo and dinosaurs won the toss. Still, we loved Bowness's lagoon with its fountain of spraying colors in the middle and the gigantic river-fed swimming pool on its north leg. Then too, it had a merry-go-round at the far east end of the park with horses that galloped much faster than the ones at the Stampede. I would have sworn. Bowness seemed to be miles from anywhere when I was a kid, and on days when I went by streetcar with friends, rather than by car with my family, travel time ate up a considerable portion of our day. Mind you, I never begrudged a streetcar ride. In the height of summer, streetcars ran from the downtown every fifteen minutes and cost ten cents, and there was a five-cent admission fee to the park.

Bowness's natural pool had a slide, which was a drawing card, but its frigid river temperature and gravel bottom was enough of a deterrent for me that I only swam there a handful of times. The lagoon rose in popularity when we reached our teens and were allowed to handle canoes on our own. Everyone headed directly for the fountain to cool off or engage in water fights with willing challengers. Extremely hot days produced a regular log jam.

The zoo was everyone's favorite, and frequently the location for year end school and church picnics. I'd like a dollar for every three-legged or sack race I ran at the zoo. And how I remember when our minister, Dr. Parsons, turned up in the dying moments of a Sunday School picnic with a gigantic bin of ice cream, waving a box of cones and a scoop. We ambushed him from all sides.

There was no entrance fee to the zoo and we loved to enter by the swinging bridge on the north side, which was an attraction itself. I'm sure there were times when Mother and Dad wondered if we ever intended to cross the bridge or just spend the day swinging it. A growling bear nearby would eventually attract our attention, and we'd head for the animals, confined in cramped cages at the east end of the park. The dinosaurs were scattered throughout the west end, but there was no prehistoric park as we know it today. We were allowed to climb all over the dinosaurs, which we did, and I remember thinking I was the king of the castle the day I ventured up the tail and back of the landmark brontosaurus at a school outing—until Roy shinnied past me all the way up Dinny's neck to his head, reducing my feat to paltry insignificance. I thought Miss Robertson was going to pass out when she saw him up there.

In the summer of '46 an appalling incident occurred at the

zoo which rocked the city and utterly devastated my mother. Donnie Goss, a sweet five-year-old, was snatched from the custody of his parents during a split second's distraction. Aghast and broken-hearted searchers later discovered his battered body hidden in the bushes. It was an unthinkable occurrence for Calgary, and forever altered Mother's relaxed demeanor at our family zoo outings.

Update:

I still glide through the coulee, but not on my skates. I'm in my car and I'm on Crowchild Trail, my beloved rink buried many feet below my wheels. The last time I saw 'Squeak' Leopold was a number of years ago at a Flames hockey game. He was driving the zamboni—in a tux—smooth as ever on ice! Pete and his popcorn disappeared in 1968.

The swimming pools are gone; the LRT now rumbles across a corner of the Crystal, and the Science Centre sits plunk on top of the Municipal.

Bowness Park and the Calgary Zoo have reversed their admission practices, with Bowness granting free admission and the Zoo charging a fee. I last rode the original Bowness merry-go-round at Heritage Park with my grandson. The horses didn't gallop as fast as they used to.

Pyjama Party.
Mary, Elaine, Me, Lois, Helen.
circa. 1954

Chapter 10

—SENIOR PURSUITS—

Uptown Girls

High school brought big changes. It was time to abandon our aimless neighborhood antics and begin cultivating more urbane, sophisticated practices. So we took to hanging out in the Bay colonnade uptown. Actually, we called it *down*town.

Suburban malls had not yet surfaced, so downtown was *the* place to shop and connect. I'd step off the Sunalta bus on the northwest corner of Eighth and First on a Saturday afternoon, stroll through the Bay colonnade, and almost assuredly, a familiar face would turn up within minutes. I bought most of my wardrobe at the Hudson's Bay, and would top off the day's purchases with a mouthwatering malt in its basement. My friend Lois tells me we used to stroll into the clock department where we'd wind and synchronize all the clocks, then set their alarms to ring in unison, while we observed the commotion from the nearby menswear. I'm reluctant to challenge her memory, but I can't imagine having done such a thing. Who, me?

I loved strolling past Liggett's Drugstore on Eighth Avenue toward the street photographer randomly capturing passersby on his camera. He aimed for candid shots and had a wonderful knack for catching his subjects during the brief moment when surrounding pedestrians cleared the frame. On a busy Saturday, it was a tough assignment, so we'd help him—without making it obvious—by jockeying for position.

Off to the movies.
Mary (in her Corey shoes) and Mike.
circa. 1954

"Slow down, there's too many people in front of us," I signal to Lois, grabbing the back of her coat. We turn and feign window shopping, while watching for an opening out of the corners of our eyes.

"There's a gap now. Quick, let's go!" We smooth our skirts, tug at our sweaters, give our hair a fast finger comb and saunter by—ever so casually.

"Would you believe that woman?" I declare indignantly. A large woman carrying a blockade of bags has stepped out of nowhere, right in front of us! We break into fits of laughter and stagger off down the street. We laugh at everything—even lost opportunities.

"Let's circle the block and try again," I suggest. We dissolve into more hysterics as we turn the corner. We have better luck stage managing the second pass. The photographer clicks and hands us our identifying ticket.

First thing after school on Monday, we return to review the results in the back of the drugstore. Hunkering over the sheet of proofs, we wrestle for possession of the magnifying glass—the all important aid for finding ourselves among the rows of postage stamp-sized images.

"There we are!" shrieks Lois. One look at the two gigglers on the photo sheet sets off the same two gigglers in the flesh. We're disappointed the photographer hasn't turned us into movie stars, so we don't buy.

But we didn't reject all his photos by any means. In fact, street photos feature largely in my meager photo collection of the time, making me especially grateful for that man. I also have an image of the photographer himself permanently imprinted on my brain—a short, stocky, balding man with a big, friendly smile, stationed behind his tri-pod, instinctively knowing when to click.

The place we spent more hours than anywhere else downtown was Heintzman's Music, located on the south side of Eighth, a beautiful store with a whole wall of closet-sized sound-proof booths for sampling the sounds of the day. Initially, we were allowed to take our selections into a booth to play on our own, but scratched records and damaged equipment forced management to introduce a system whereby the clerks piped our requests in from a central system.

"This new arrangement is lousy," Lois complains.

"I'll bet the clerks don't like it any better than we do," I agree.

But we aren't about to let the new system interfere with our Saturday entertainment, so we step in and out of our booth every two minutes all afternoon, requisitioning one record after another—until we have sampled the entire week's hit parade.

"We'd better buy at least one," I murmur, a little embarrassed at monopolizing the end booth all afternoon. I step up to the desk and fork over 99 cents for a '78' of Johnny Ray's *Cry*, an appropriate selection considering the state of the clerk serving me.

We always bought singles, either 78 rpm's or the smaller, lighter 45's which had a nuisancy large hole in the middle requiring either a different stem on the record player or little snap-in discs to alter the hole. Long playing 33's were out of our price range and never that popular with the high school crowd.

A visit downtown was never complete without stopping at the Nut House, next to the Palace Theater. The Nut House had devised a brilliant marketing scheme, a guarantee in lights, "If we fail to smile, your purchase free." The smell of the nuts was temptation enough, but the thought of engineering a free pound of cashews through the clerk failing to smile was irresistible. I hate to think how many nuts we ate—and begrudgingly paid for—through our failed attempts. Management clearly didn't hire anyone who suffered from PMS or experienced bad hair days.

The high school gang's favorite eating spot was The Skyline, one of the few hangouts that wasn't downtown. In fact, it was located about as far from town as you could get, seemingly miles from anywhere. In reality, it was located at the north end of where Chinook Centre sits today, but little existed in the stretch between there and the Stampede Grounds.

The Skyline, depicted with amazing accuracy in the popular sitcom of the seventies, *Happy Days,* had both car service outside and table service inside. Early on, the proprietors discovered the need for a traffic controller to prevent inside patrons from parking in the area designated for car service, so they hired an earnest little Englishman, who they dressed in an oversized uniform and instructed to intercept every car as it approached.

"Is youse wishin' coib soivice?" he'd ask, flagging you to a stop and poking his head in your window. I'd stifle the giggles every time I saw him coming. But I was horrified the time my date saw him coming, leaned out the window and offered, "Yessuh, we's wishin' coib soivice." What a relief when I realized our little warden was blissfully unaware he'd been ridiculed!

The Skyline had a couple of other attachments, a CKXL broadcast booth manned by the popular disk jockey Ted Soskin, and a golf driving range out behind, which we used only occasionally. The main attraction for me was definitely the "coib soivice." A plain hamburger at the Skyline cost 40 cents, a bowl of chili 45 cents and a milkshake 25 cents. Coffee or a coke was 10 cents, but there was a whopping 25 cent cover charge for car or table service. Menus also stated in bold block letters, WE DO NOT CATER TO DRINKING PARTIES, specifying in brackets (We do not serve mixer or ice)—no doubt to discourage patrons from carting in their own booze, which no restaurant was licensed to serve.

Then south of the Skyline, way, way out in the boonies, we used to gather for wiener roasts at a place we called Paradise Grove. The area was inhabited by squatters who had the audacity to construct a gate across the road and charge us an entrance fee. We knew they had no right to do this, but acquiesced knowing our 50 cents was probably the extent of their income for the week. Paradise Grove would have been in the area we now know as Fish Creek Park.

Theaters

Like most kids, I preferred the company of my friends for amusement outings, yet I frequently reserved the movie theater for my family, no doubt lured by Dad's great love for stage and screen, which he enthusiastically introduced us to at an early age.

For a period, the King family were regular Saturday evening patrons of Calgary's downtown theaters, our favorites being the Grand, the Palace and the Capitol—the Grand on First Street West between Sixth and Seventh Avenues and the Palace and Capitol across the street from one another on Eighth Avenue, between First and Second Streets West. Each had originally been designed for live stage as well as film, so they were ornately decorated—too beautiful, I used to think, to be plunged into darkness.

The theaters had balconies where all the smokers sat, creating a gray haze which hung menacingly over the seating area. With the exception of major blockbusters, movies ran continuously without the theater being cleared between showings, so ushers escorted us to seats by flashlight whatever time we arrived. Not infrequently, people arrived in the middle of a movie, and simply stayed until that frame rolled around again. My family aimed for a movie's beginning, but if we arrived early and decided to secure seats right away, Don and I would avoid the climax by putting our heads in our laps and plugging our ears until Dad signaled it was safe to come up. Dad got to see endings twice.

Every movie was accompanied by previews of coming attractions, a cartoon—Bugs Bunny, Elmer Fudd, Gerald McBoing-Boing or our favorite, the Near-sighted McGoo—and the Movietone News, with endless depressing footage of the war. The musicals of the time were designed to lift war-weary spirits, and we also lapped up clips of the latest fashion trends or the Royal Family on its most recent excursion. *God Save the King* lit up the screen at the close of every evening, and we stood reverently until its conclusion. We won't forget the night the news featured the death of our beloved King George VI, nor the shock of rising that first time for *God Save the* Queen.

The Grand, part of the Orpheum circuit, was Calgary's oldest theater, built by Senator James Lougheed in 1912 as a vaudeville house. At its inception it was ranked the finest in Western Canada with a large stage, plush velvet curtains, stunning cantilevered balcony, brass rails, private boxes and ornate carvings. Dad always talked about the good old days when a bevy of internationally acclaimed stars performed in "The Showcase of Alberta," as it was dubbed—Vilma Banky, Sir John Martin Harvey, Sophie Tucker, George Burns & Gracie Allen, Fred Astaire, The Marx Brothers and Sarah Bernhardt—the "Divine Miss Sarah." The Grand also housed the original Calgary Symphony Orchestra, under the direction of Clayton Hare in the forties, later amalgamating with the Alberta Philharmonic to form the Calgary Philharmonic Orchestra we know today.

Paul Robeson, the African American baritone took the city by storm when he performed at the Grand in 1946. Many Calgarians were ecstatic to have a singer of his stature gracing their stage, while others, insecure with his color, were less welcoming. Still others were downright outraged to have a man known for left-wing political activism in their midst.

The live event I best remember at the Grand Theater was the touring *Passion Play*, which I attended with my Sunalta School class in about grade five or six. The elaborate production, from South Dakota I believe, bowled me over, and I never got over seeing real live camels and donkeys on stage, or the unthinkable scene-stealing performance of one shockingly crude camel that irreverently relieved itself on center stage—in the Grand Theater yet!

The Palace was built in 1921, also as a vaudeville and movie house, and was Calgary's largest theater with seating capacity for 1,968 people. In fact, for a time, it was the largest single screen house in Canada. Mother and Dad were great fans of Bible Bill Aberhart and his *Back to the Bible Hour* broadcast from the "Station of the Calgary Herald," quartered at the Palace. Years later, I listened to Clarence Mack's Saturday morning *Good Deed*

Radio Club from the same station. And for a period there was a live Saturday morning *Mickey Mouse Club* where ten cents got us a talent show, sing songs, cartoon and serial. The family also attended some wonderful live musicals from the Palace stage, *Oklahoma* being one that knocked my socks off. I sang *Surrey with the Fringe on Top* for weeks afterward.

An especially memorable series our family attended was the 1950/51 Celebrity Concerts: four evenings which featured the remarkable unsighted pianist, Alec Templeton; George London, a bass baritone; Jan Peerce, the famous tenor; and Charles Laughton, renowned British actor. Jan Peerce made a practice of reserving his signature song, *Bluebird of Happiness*, for an encore, a performer's strategy unfamiliar to us at the time. When he invited requests from the audience, Don leapt from his seat and cried "BLUEBIRD!" Peerce obliged, of course, and we floated on cloud nine presuming he was singing it just for us. When the evening featuring Charles Laughton rolled around, I balked at attending. An entire evening of readings was unfathomable, and I was convinced he'd be a crashing bore. How wrong I was. He had me mesmerized from his first utterance to his last, and in fact, he turned out to be my undisputed favorite of the four.

At the conclusion of every concert, Don and I bolted from our seats and sprinted backstage for autographs, successfully procuring all four. I'll never forget approaching Charles Laughton, trembling from head to toe at the very thought of breathing the same air as this formidable icon. Stretching on tiptoe, I reached my program up over his enormous girth and timidly croaked, "Please, sir," feeling like Oliver raising his bowl to Mr. Bumble. Then I cowered in his shadow bracing for the expected rebuff. But suddenly, the program was snatched from my fingers, and he was scribbling furiously across its face before turning gruffly toward my brother, and obliging him alike. Then, with his manager dancing attendance, he whirled on his heel and strode purposefully toward the exit. As we watched his great, wobbling jowls disappear from sight, we heard him grumble, "Jolly little nuisances!"

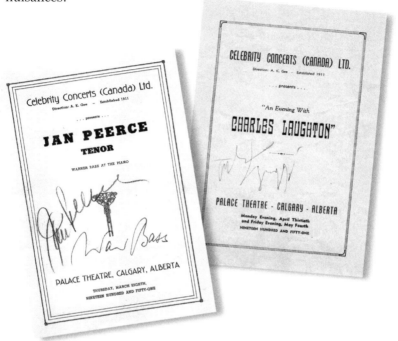

The Capitol Theater was the most ornate of the three theaters and, hands down, my favorite. I felt completely at home in the Capitol, and still dream about its long, regal interior staircase that magically set the mood for an evening's entertainment. There was a cramped coat check adjacent to the canteen, and I don't remember anyone but the same gray haired woman at its helm for the life of the place. Mother and Dad always left their coats with her and she always greeted them by name. I also remember exquisite architectural decorating, fancy loges, elegant washrooms and smartly uniformed ushers.

Dad knew the manager, Ralph Mitcheltree, and on rare occasions imposed on him with a request for seats when he knew opening night of a major film would place them at a premium. Mr. Mitcheltree could be counted on to greet us at the top of the stairs, then personally deliver us to selected seats, a favoritism I accepted with gratitude, but a degree of embarrassment. I was able to rationalize the privilege, however, with the premise that the King family was conceivably keeping the Capitol afloat single-handedly.

On Saturdays, as young kids, we used to walk down Seventeenth Avenue to the Kinema Theater at the bottom of the hill on Fourteenth Street, where 20 cents got us a double feature, cartoon and serial, plus popcorn. Because parents were rarely in attendance, the long, narrow theater was in eternal chaos with a steady flow of kids arriving, departing, or parading back and forth to the canteen, not to mention flicking popcorn across the aisles. The truth of the matter is, it was such bedlam, I never liked it very much myself.

The first of the drive-ins arrived in 1949, and at one time the city boasted seven of them. They were received with great enthusiasm as an economical outing for frugal families and an undisturbed parking lot for torrid teens. They had a number of drawbacks, however: cars could get uncomfortably cold if the weather was inclement, although some drive-ins enticed customers with offers of free heaters; show times could be very late, especially during summer solstice when it took forever to grow dark; the crackling speakers produced appalling sounds, thanks in part to regularly being ripped from their stands when drivers pulled away with them still attached to the car window; and windshields constantly fogged up, either from rain or a carload of breathers, heavy or otherwise.

I won't forget the night I went to the drive-in with three girlfriends, and a carload of four boys wheeled into the spot directly behind us. After much honking and sign language, some members of both parties agreed to a foreign exchange. When two willing participants from our car made the first move, the two of us left behind, dubious of the scheme, lunged for the locks and barred all collaborators. Then for the entire double feature, we smugly chuckled in comfort while the conglomerate behind fought for territory in a fogged up rattletrap. The incredible conclusion to the story is that a pairing emerged from that fateful night, and proceeded through a brief courtship directly to the altar. The marriage produced four spectacular children, but alas, didn't make it to the closing credits.

Radio and Television

Radio was our exclusive at-home entertainment and captivated us by the hour with everything from comedy and drama, to music, sports and soaps, all performed brilliantly by mysterious voices we attached to imaginary faces. The mystery voices were accompanied by a supporting cast of ingenious sound effects, which played a major role in the success of productions.

After school I'd curl up in Dad's big green chair by the radio with an apple and a glass of milk and turn the dial to *Dinah Shore* and the *Bob Crosby Show*. The soaps, *Pepper Young's Family* or *Ma Perkins*, were strictly daytime, so we could only tune in if we were home from school sick—a rare occurrence for me. After supper, there was a nightly string of programs that competed with homework assignments for my attention, and we all know who won. I might have attempted to solve an algebra problem with the *Green Hornet* or *Boston Blackie* skulking in the background, but I lowered my pencil when the deep, menacing voice of John

Archer intoned, "Who knows what evil lurks in the hearts of men? *The Shadow* knows."

Comedies took up a lion's share of the airwaves with the likes of *Wayne & Shuster*—not nearly as funny in the medium of television—*Bob Hope, Fibber McGee & Molly,* and a back-to-back string on Sundays beginning at 4:00 p.m. with *Our Miss Brooks* followed by *Fred Allen, Edgar Bergen & Charlie McCarthy, Jack Benny* and *Amos 'N Andy*. Weekends also delivered two musical favorites, the *Hit Parade* on Saturdays and in sharp contrast, The *Leslie Bell Singers* on Sunday, a magnificent all-female chorus broadcast from Winnipeg. And backing up to the forties, who could forget our local librarian extraordinaire, Louise Riley, in a class by herself, delivering her Saturday morning story to a widespread audience of rapt children.

But the *pièce de résistance* in our household of movie buffs was Monday night's *Lux Radio Theater*, adaptations of films in current release, broadcast live from New York with the Hollywood lead stars playing their original roles, supported by a Broadway cast. We used to think a film's box office must suffer once such brilliantly directed radio adaptations had been aired, but the Hollywood studios claimed otherwise. The productions, in fact, provided good promotion for their films.

Television made its debut some time during my high school years, but Dad wouldn't hear of having a set in the home to run interference with my studies. Our household must have held some kind of a record for resisting TV, yet I don't remember feeling deprived. Radio was providing a perfectly satisfactory distraction. Then our Aunt Mildred got a television set, and guess who was first in line to check it out? Dad was on Aunt Mildred's front porch before she got it plugged in; not to be denied, the rest of us were right on his heels. We were a comical sight that first night.

"Mom, it's coming on," Cousin Frank calls to his mother, busying about in the kitchen.

"I'm just making some tea. I'll be right there," she sings, assuring him she'll be ready in time.

"But you'll miss the start," he worries. It's Sunday night, and we're sitting in a ring around Aunt Mildred's big comfy living room, eyes glued to her grand console TV stationed solemnly in the corner, its blank screen now flickering to life.

"Never mind the tea, Mildred," Dad calls in a panic, "you mustn't miss Ed." By this time the screen is flecked with snow and crackling with static. Then bang! . . . bang, bang! A spray of fireworks explodes, and Aunt Mildred scurries to her chair, just in time, as . . . Ed Sullivan steps into the room!

Ed's fans gathered every Sunday night for some weeks—same time, same place—to watch in disbelief, as *Toast of the Town* magically burst forth from a screen that largely lay dormant the rest of the time. Dad absolutely loved Ed Sullivan's grab bag of variety acts, and remained a fan for life. "No one has ever held a candle to Ed," he contended to his dying day. I still chuckle at the memory of Dad's grim determination to resist television all those years, except on Sunday nights when we'd beat a path to Aunt Mildred's house to see Ed Sullivan's "Re-e-e-l-ly Big Sh-o-o-o."

Mewata Stadium

Mewata Stadium was the city's one conventional venue for football and track, its turf shared by the schools and the Calgary Stampeder football team. I remember my brother Stan taking me to my first professional football game when I was eleven years old, patiently explaining all the rules so I'd know what was happening on the field. As luck would have it, the year was 1948, the legendary year that Calgary won its first Grey Cup, beating

Ottawa 10-7, and needless to say, football won a new young fan.

As I recall the Grey Cup events of that year, 300 or so boisterous fans traveled by train across the country to cheer their team to victory, arguably upstaging it by streaming into Toronto *en masse* and turning it on its heels. Union Station shook with wall-to-wall square dancers, while the Royal York Hotel braced in expectation of their onslaught. Cowboys stomped the streets, flapjacks flipped from chuckwagons, and Don Mackay, Calgary's flamboyant goodwill ambassador—soon to be mayor—paraded on horseback down Younge Street waving his white hat. Calgarians stole the hearts of the entire country, and even won the affection of the Royal York Hotel, which invited them back the next year. The Grey Cup puffed home in the arms of its jubilant supporters to thousands of screaming fans awaiting at the station. Don Mackay's white hat became Calgary's adopted trademark, and any Calgarian old enough to remember will tell you that it was Calgary's 1948 trans Canada trainload of revelers that made the Grey Cup the national festival it is today.

Stan departed for university the September following our first games together, but I continued to attend with friends, some who made it a habit to enter Mewata over or through the fence, and not always successfully. Only now that my mother is safely in her grave will I confess to the ruse my friend Elaine and I devised. We'd hang around Mewata's entrance gates until we spotted a suitable candidate for a surrogate father, favoring a big, blustery cigar-chomping type who was drawing a lot of attention his way. Then we'd slip in front of him and, sticking like glue, edge toward the gates as he did. On reaching a gate—and in the absence of turnstiles—we'd move quickly through, the ticket taker assuming "Dad," bringing up the rear, held *three* tickets. By the time he discovered otherwise, we had vanished into the crowd and he couldn't leave his post to give chase. Whenever that still small voice nagged me about our underhanded entry, I clung to the rationale that climbing over or through the fence bordered on corrupt, but walking through the gate in plain sight? Is it my fault no one asked me for a ticket? Besides, we never took up a seat, nor did we want one. Even when Elaine's *real* father treated us to a game, we'd immediately abandon our reserved seats, and camp on the sidelines as near to the players' bench as we dared creep. If we played our cards right, we could get breathtakingly close.

I pursued the Stampeders every inch of the way that season, attending every game, cheering for the red and white and scrambling for autographs from my enviable sideline position. After the Western final, we kids all stormed the field and toppled the goal posts, after which a mob of guys with jackknives converged like locusts to gouge souvenir samples. I couldn't wait to get home and tape my prized splinter to my dresser mirror above my photos of Keith Spaith and Sugarfoot Anderson. Needless to say, I was part of the mob at the train station for the celebrated Grey Cup party's send-off, and again for their triumphant return. I continued to attend games throughout the Mewata years, occasionally even supporting the team with the purchase of a ticket.

For some reason, baseball wasn't a big attraction for my circle of friends, so the only time I remember visiting Buffalo Stadium— where Eau Claire is situated today—was with my friend Barbara, whose big brother was a pitcher. Likewise, I only went to the occasional Big Six hockey game at the Victoria Arena, and then usually on a Sunday when the law forbade charging admission. Getting in for a silver collection, however, wasn't nearly as satisfying as sailing in on chutzpah.

Update:

In 1972 The Grand Theater, housed in the Lougheed Building, was converted to a side-by-side twin cinema, its beautiful cantilevered balcony sliced in half. Then, alas, the lights dimmed for the last time on November 22, 1999. Some time after that, a Golf Centre invaded the premises, and the working crowd—with no more reverence than that camel—spend their lunch hours ripping balls into a net. Demolition threatened the Lougheed Building from the eighties until early 2003, when Neil Richardson, of Heritage Property Corporation, purchased the building with an eye to restoring its facade, and preserving any historically significant portions of its interior.

The Calgary Philharmonic Orchestra moved to the Jubilee Auditorium in 1957, then to its current home, the Jack Singer concert Hall in 1985.

The Palace Theater closed in 1990, and loitered in uncertainty until 1996 when it was designated a Provincial Historic Resource. A 4.1 million dollar restoration returned it to its former grandeur, and in 1998, its doors re-opened as a nightclub.

My beloved Capitol Theater is just a ghost, having been swept aside for the Scotia Center development in 1992.

The Kinema Theater disappeared in the mid fifties.

It's hard to believe that my favorite Cinema Park Drive-in used to sprawl over the 22 hectares of land on Memorial Drive now occupied by Point McKay. The Corral, the last surviving drive-in, folded in August, 1999 when an explosion at the nearby Hub Oil recycling plant damaged its fading screen.

Mewata Stadium was torn down in 1999 to make way for Shaw Millennium Park, a skateboarding extravaganza, which opened September 30, 2000.

Chapter 11

−DOUBLE FEATURE−

The Calgary Stampede

As school wound to a halt each summer, the Calgary Stampede was always waiting in the wings to capture our attention. The Stampede ran for just six days then, beginning with Monday morning's parade, and closing with a packed midway of last-chance rollickers at midnight on Saturday. Operating anything of the sort on Sunday was unthinkable. Mother used to say that Grandpa Anderson proclaimed July 12—a date that inevitably fell during Stampede week—to be Calgary's hottest day of the year. It often was.

Monday morning of parade day inevitably dawned clear and bright, and the excitement in the air was palpable as crowds lining the parade route grew to four, five and six deep. Dad's Seventh Avenue restaurant was made-to-order for the event, launching us with a hearty Stampede breakfast, then providing box seats atop its single story roof for perfect viewing. The instability of the Tea Kettle Inn's roof gave Dad the jitters, however, and he chewed his nails through every parade fearing someone would fall right through and land on the soda fountain below.

Our caretaker, affectionately nicknamed "Becksy," loyally manned the ladder he'd secured at the back of the restaurant. "Single file down the side," he'd repeat—boss's orders—as he gave the ladies a hand from the ladder onto the roof, and one at a time, we'd gingerly pick our way along the perimeter to the front ledge. Becksy always missed the parade himself, standing guard throughout to prevent gate crashers from storming the roof. He rejected the option of pulling up the ladder, not to be denied his once-a-year position of authority.

"I'll be right back," said Dad hurriedly one parade morning, as he ignored his own rules by making a sudden, inexplicable dash—directly across the *middle* of the roof—for the ladder. Becksy jumped to attention to steady it as Dad skittered to the bottom in record time.

"What's going on?" we asked Mother, as we searched the scene below for a possible clue. We quickly discovered the answer. Directly below, a spectator had collapsed with heatstroke, and Dad was already administering emergency medical service with a cold drink. Although the restaurant was closed during the parade, Dad brought his wobbly patient inside until he was fully recovered, then both returned to their viewing stands. I remember repeat scenarios of this on other parade mornings.

Meanwhile, Aunt Lil had other concerns. "Audrey, you *must* sit still. If you keep running around like that, you'll crash right through the roof and Uncle Horace will be very cross!" Of course, her *real* concern was that her exuberant child would cartwheel *off* the roof. Eventually, Aunt Lil took control of the matter in her typical forthright fashion. Little Audrey watched the parade tied to the flagpole.

We all had our favorite section of the parade, with Mother winning the prize for the most bewildering selection. We couldn't imagine why anyone would light up at the sight of Old Timer's wagons. Mother would begin rattling off one name after another as the wagons rolled by, her eyes darting from face to face in instant recognition. She knew every one. For me, it was the marching bands, especially the high stepping majorettes with their shimmering sequins and flying batons. I harbored an unfulfilled dream of being a majorette for years. At the very least, I should be assured of a seat on an Old Timer's carriage one day. I know Mother will smile and wave.

The evening grandstand show differed considerably from the shows familiar to us today. The shows were created mainly from a string of imported variety acts—as though we had a pipeline to the Ed Sullivan Show—with nothing like the Young Canadians to tie them together. But they worked, and everyone loved them. There were usually a number of animal acts, and they ranked the highest on the popularity list. Concluding fireworks dazzled the crowds then as they do today.

The midway was assembled on an acreage of sawdust and wood shavings, which must have been a challenge for workers to spread and later clean away, but it made a splendid carpet for sore feet. The midway carried some seedy sideshows which, looking back, must have been rather shocking for Alberta's bible belt. Two that come to mind are *Harlem in Havana*, an all black musical/dance revue, supposedly of considerable talent, and *Club Lido*, a sleazy girlie show of questionable talent. Mother always claimed the best part of the midway could be seen free on the outside, and she was always right, although I'm quite certain she never tested her theory on Club Lido.

She wouldn't have been caught dead gawking up at the Lido lovelies lining the outdoor stage, clasping their soiled, threadbare capes around their shoulders, daring onlookers to ponder the treasures underneath. My friends and I, lacking Mother's sophistication, loved watching the barkers work the crowd, luring potential customers with their ever escalating pitches timed to climax with the onstage temptresses spinning on their heels and vanishing through the tent flap with a final naughty flip of their capes. Then the crowd would disperse, most onlookers satisfied they'd seen the best there was to offer, leaving only a handful of oglers lined up at the ticket booth hungry for more. I hope they weren't disappointed.

Another famous attraction of the time was the *Freak Show*, a gauche spectacle displaying victims of birth defects like animals in a zoo. It was one of the midway's big drawing cards. The disgrace was eventually deemed "politically incorrect" and banished from the site. Gambling operated under a double standard: an actual casino was unthinkable, but individual booths scattered up and down the midway operated freely with little attention paid to age restrictions. Finally, we ended the big week with one last trip to the grounds on Sunday to watch the carney workers dismantle the rides, an operation that still amazes me. But there was another reason for our Sunday visit—to kick through the sawdust in search of dropped change. It was rarely lucrative, but, like gambling, the anticipation of unearthing a jackpot kept us coming back.

And lastly, who could forget October 18, 1951—the day a condensed "Special Stampede" was produced for our visiting Princess Elizabeth and her dashing Prince Philip as they huddled under a magnificent Hudson's Bay point blanket in their white stetsons. I missed the entire performance because my eyes were riveted on the couple from Camelot.

Halloween

Halloween delivered the same excitement then as it does today, except there were no repetitive racks of common, flimsy costumes dangling unappealingly in every retail outlet in town. Half the fun was unleashing our imaginations to create our own originals, then scrounging through closets and drawers for the required ingredients. I must confess, however, there was one year

I couldn't resist my Aunt Millie's offer to raid her trunk brimming with *real* costumes from my grandfather's stage endeavors.

"This gypsy costume will fit you," Aunt Millie suggested, as she held up an authentic looking peasant blouse and ankle-length, jagged-edged skirt. I pulled them on and twirled before her mirror. "Oh my, you're a wonderful gypsy!" she enthused. Then she dug deep into the

Mask Designers. Jeanette, Elaine, Helen, Me. circa. 1948

trunk and brought up more bracelets than I could imagine. As I skipped up her stairs, they jangled from my wrists to my elbows.

Aunt Millie, who remained childless, though not by choice, loved the opportunity Halloween provided for contact with kids. I'll never forget the year she donned a gypsy costume—*my* gypsy costume—and received starry-eyed trick-or-treaters in Aunt Lil's dimly lit kitchen. Aunt Lil spent the night directing each one of us around to her back door.

The gypsy gazed into the glowing crystal ball intently, then after a long pause, "Aha, I see a long life for you—a long and happy life." She was the talk of the block, and I never revealed her identity to my awestruck friends. They believed the seer's every promising prediction.

We confined our Halloweening to Scarboro, but never called it a day until we'd hit every last house in the neighborhood. Our parents never accompanied us, even when we were very little, and everyone managed to turn up in one piece at the end of the day. I began with a direct run across the street to the Mason's. Mrs. Mason, the sweetest woman on earth, made the most scrumptious

Our Halloween "tricking" dummy.
Joan, Me, Helen, Margaret, Mr. Dummy, Mary, Catharine, Elaine. circa. 1950

popcorn balls on earth, and they went fast. To this day, a
Halloween never goes by that I don't think of Mrs. Mason. We
collected our candy in pillowcases, and made a pit stop at half
time to dump our booty onto our beds before heading back out for
a fresh start. Sometimes I used this intermission to brave a
second go at the Mason's on the off chance there was one
lingering popcorn ball. Not a chance! I ate every lick of my loot
within the week. Don's suckers and kisses rotted in his closet until
the next Halloween.

For a period during the war, we collected "savings stamps,"
much as kids today collect money for UNICEF. The stamps
represented the amount of money purchasers had donated to
assist the war effort. The schools became involved by offering
prizes for classes collecting the most, so we got very competitive,
which meant parents had to rise to the occasion by purchasing
more stamps. My eyes popped out of my head when my kitchen
gypsy tore off an entire strip of stamps, and slipped it into my bag.
No wonder she was so confident in foretelling a happy life for me!

Chapter 12

–THE MAIN EVENT–

Christmas

My childhood Christmases were a dream, but as the years passed, it became more and more apparent, that for Mother, the season was closer to being a nightmare. The chronic fatigue that had dogged her for as long as we could remember, eventually developed into full blown clinical depressions, their mystifying, erratic comings and goings frequently throwing her—and us—off balance. But as Christmas approached, a depression striking—in its most incapacitating form—was as reliable as Santa landing on our rooftop. Our family celebrated Christmas on a teeter totter, with four of us flying on the high end, reveling in the family's favorite traditions, and Mother, seemingly handcuffed to the low end, fighting a losing battle to get off the ground.

Fortunately, Dad possessed a festive euphoria that nothing could dampen and it went a long way to counter-balance Mother's inertia. We were all sympathetic toward her situation, yet silently resolved to preserve our traditions with or without her sanctions. It frequently meant delicately over-ruling her appeals to reduce or simplify.

"Just get a nice little decorative tree we can sit on a table in the window," she'd plead, as Dad and I headed out the door for the opening tradition of the season—always on the coldest day of the year, I swear. Mother, one foot out the door, would demonstrate her fuss-free vision by holding her hand two feet above the step, and nodding agreement, we'd jump into the car and set forth on our tree hunt. Two hours later we'd return with a whopper, and Dad would have to lop off at least a foot to keep it from scraping the ceiling. Mother would heave a sigh, but resist an all-out complaint. It was Christmas, after all. We were secretly pleased the year Aunt Mildred rejected Mother's proposal to dispense with the gift giving amongst the cousins. *"Yea, Aunt Mildred!"* Mother should have known better than to broach her, of all people, with such a motion—Aunt Mildred was Christmas personified.

Dad was extremely resourceful, so we often found second hand items under the tree—skis, skates or toboggans that he'd polished to an inviting new shine. New or used, every gift was new to me, and I'd wolf down my breakfast so I could get to the coulee to try out my exciting *new* gear. I wouldn't return until it was time for turkey. My very first wrist watch was second hand, stuffed into the toe of my stocking. I was safely past Santa age, and recognized it as an item that had lived forever in the fascinating trinket drawer of Mother's dresser—a treasured memento left by her mother. It was a tarnished old timepiece with no strap and no tick. Dad had called upon his watch-making skills to restore it to its former glory, if not beyond. I loved my shiny *new* watch, and the priceless gift that accompanied it—an attachment through time to the grandmother I never knew.

Dining Room Pool Hall

I remember there being one Christmas—only one—that kept me home all day. It began as usual, with the flurry around the tree, except this year when the last present was opened, and we surveyed our riches, I became painfully aware that Stan's allotment was extremely meager. *"How come Don and I got more than Stan?"* I wondered. *"No fair, he's such a nice brother."* True to character, Stan was entirely disregarding the inequity, charitably finding joy in the happiness of his younger siblings. As we scooped up the last of the wrapping paper, Mother called us for breakfast, and we stepped into the dining room—to utter pandemonium!

There, parked on the dining room table was a gift "To Stan, from Santa"—a pool table—with dull pads, sagging pockets, a triangle of rickety balls, and a scarred cue poised for the break. It was beautiful! The legless relic was at least second hand—more likely third or fourth—but the smile it brought to Stan's face was priceless. Mother threw in the towel on breakfast; I scrapped my traditional coulee excursion; and only when the extended family was due to arrive for dinner did we reluctantly gather up the balls and pack the table down to its rightful place in the rumpus room. It was the best Christmas ever!

Christmas dinner was classic Norman Rockwell, celebrated with all our cousins, wearing our Sunday best. The man of the house carved the golden turkey on a grand platter at the head of the table, and the plates traveled clockwise to the lady of the house who served helpings of steaming vegetables from elegant tureens at the opposite end. I loved watching Dad give the carving knife its annual honing, rhythmically swiping each side of the blade up and down the sharpening steel. He turned it into quite a workout. Looking back on our Christmas dinners I see a lovely balance between formal decorum and relaxed joviality. I don't see a drop of alcohol at the table, but its absence most assuredly did not stifle chatter or laughter.

After dinner we laughed our heads off over raucous games the entire evening. When the bell struck midnight, those departing for home donned their outerwear, then we all lingered at the front door chatting and laughing some more because we couldn't bear to part company. Christmases were so-o-o-o good.

The Branches of our Christmas Tree

Last photo of Uncle Harry as he was leaving for Edmonton to undergo brain surgery. 1947

How I wish my memories of Christmases down the street at '420' included more of Uncle Harry. He was every kid's dream of a dad and uncle with his fun-loving, imaginative mind, unending patience, apparent indifference to discipline, and surprises in his pockets. He absolutely loved kids and we kids instinctively knew it.

I've never forgotten the Christmas Uncle Harry had us fish for our presents. "Come on kids, let's go fishing," he grinned, leading us two at a time to the pond—a sheet draped high above our heads across a corner of the kitchen. He outfitted each of us with our very own rod, fashioned from a stick with a line of string dangling from the end, and attached to that, the all-important hook—a safety pin. Then he studiously gave us a "how to" lesson in fishing with the same patience to detail that he taught tennis. While Aunt Lil distracted us with a practice session, he slipped behind the sheet to await the fishermen. We cast our lines over the net, using perfect form as we'd been taught, and the action began.

"I got a bite!" I shrieked at Ritchie, frantically flipping my line up and over the sheet, only to flop an empty safety pin at my feet. "Wha-a-?"

"Oh dear," lamented Aunt Lil, "it got away. Never mind, at least we know there's a fish in there. Try again." I cast again, and the crouching fish nibbled and teased until he sensed I was about to explode with excitement, then with a mighty tug, he struck!

"You've got one this time," yelled Ritchie, dropping his own rod and grabbing mine, tossing it skyward and proudly landing my fish—the most amazing fish I'd ever seen—a Greer Garson coloring book, wrapped in bright red tissue paper bound with green ribbon. I never knew anyone else who got to go fishing at Christmas.

Aunt Lil.
circa. 1928

I also remember Uncle Harry holding a "guess the baby's weight" contest at a staff Christmas party, comically placing little Audrey, then 4-5 months old, on the restaurant's big butcher scales after all the guesses had been recorded. And lastly, I remember climbing the steps to '420' that first heartbreaking Christmas after Uncle Harry had gone, wondering how on earth we could possibly celebrate the day, or any Christmas thereafter, without him. But Aunt Lil bravely rose to the occasion. Young, resilient hearts heal quickly, and laughter reigned as always—just as Uncle Harry would have wanted.

Aunt Lil, widowed at age forty, carried on gamely, providing for her family in the familiar surroundings of their Scarboro home. She returned to her teaching career and pulled us all through the

monumental adjustment of our terrible loss. Marion, at twelve, reaped the greatest benefits from her father's legacy, while Ritchie, at eight, was denied critical boyhood years with a dad, and little Audrey, only three, was abandoned in a void. It breaks my heart to think that Audrey has no memory of streaking down the hill into her dad's open arms as he appeared around the corner on his walk home from work—an indelible memory for the rest of us.

On the town with our double cuzzes.
Upper: Aud, Me, Ritchie. circa. 1955
Lower: Mar, Don. circa. 1956

Christmases at the inviting Elbow Park home of Uncle Walter's family were unbeatable. We particularly looked forward to the years our rotating party delivered us there. But from 1950 on, Uncle Walter's empty chair was a constant reminder that one more irreplaceable member of our family was missing, and things would never be the same. My only two blood uncles—gone in less than four years—and I was only thirteen years old. I was old enough, however, to recognize how blessed I'd been to have had them, even for this short time, and a Christmas never passed that I wasn't keenly aware of their presence.

I remember Uncle Walter as a high energy, intense man who I was always a little afraid of, yet conversely, drawn to like a magnet. In contrast, Aunt Mildred was a quiet, gentle soul whose family, church and community constantly reaped the benefit of her loving touch. Cousins Art and Frank were boisterous, fun loving jokesters who teased their older sister Ethel mercilessly. I sometimes wondered if they thought that was their sole purpose in life. My early recollections of Ethel revolve around her collection of shoes that would have been the envy of Imelda Marcos, one pair having lights in the heels that turned on with each step.

Uncle Walter & Aunt Mildred.
September 2, 1926

Art, Ethel, Frank. circa. 1945

She also had a library of party games second to none. When the Walter King family arrived in Calgary after the war, I don't mind admitting I was a bit apprehensive about these strangers entering the only clan I knew, our tight little circle of double cousins. But it was love at first sight, and Hallelujah, they doubled my cousins!

The festooned home of Uncle Walter and Aunt Mildred received us with open arms, and its expansive living and dining rooms were just the ticket for all our antics. Aunt Mildred's gorgeous hand made Christmas decorations dripped from every wall, mantle and tabletop—even the toilet seat. It was a feast for the eyes. The immense dining room table was covered with an exquisite, seasonal tablecloth, every delicate motif and sequin meticulously stitched by her tender hands. And on top of that was a banquet beyond imagining.

An elegant silver tea service, polished to a gleaming shine, rested at one end of the table before a pleasing collection of fine china cups and saucers. At the other end, there'd be a mile high sandwich loaf, much too beautifully decorated to cut into, but we did anyway. Then in-between, every remaining square inch was taken up with platters of heavenly delectables that never dwindled even though we snapped them up like locusts as we circled again and again.

"Do you think that's the last Goosnargh cake?" I whisper to Mar. "I shouldn't take the last one."

"Are you kidding?" Mar laughs, "Aunt Mildred never runs out of anything, least of all Goosnargh cakes." So I reach for the lone surviving cookie beckoning from the middle of the plate, and magically, a whole fresh plate of these plump, round shortbreads, stuffed with caraway seeds and topped with a mountain of powdered sugar, appears out of nowhere. Marion shoots me a what-did-I-tell-you grin.

If you haven't had one of my Aunt Mildred's trademark Goosnargh cakes—a secret recipe my Aunt Millie especially purchased for her in England—you haven't lived. The neat part about them was they were served with a side attraction—the Goosnargh Gambol—composed and directed by Cousins Art and Frank. It went like this: at the precise moment you bit down on your powdered delight, my cousins would break into roll-on-the-floor fits of laughter, causing you to blow the top layer of powdered sugar all over yourself; then, as you gasped for breath, you'd inhale the next layer and choke to death. Their favorite victim was Stan, who they could count on for a Charlie Chaplin performance of coughing, choking, gagging, and powdering his navy blue suit from collar to cuff, giving them license to haul out the vacuum cleaner and attack him with the hose. In the end, we all took a powder, and I'm wondering if poor Aunt Mildred didn't have to vacuum her ceiling after we left.

The Walter King family also had a tradition of hit and run gift delivery. Our doorbell would ring any given evening in the week leading up to Christmas, and we'd open the door to find presents mysteriously perched on the front steps, while loud guffaws emanated from a familiar car, its tail lights fading from view down the street. We still talk about the year our restaurant had been robbed at gunpoint, and two days before Christmas, a giant box with a stick strangely poking up through the lid greeted us from the top step. An attached note read, "This is a stick up." Only the Walter Kings!

Dad's only sister, Aunt Millie, and our Uncle 'D' lived in a charming little retirement bungalow on Britannia Drive, a sanctuary they'd designed in detail for their subdued, child-free lifestyle. We wisely

Uncle 'D' & Aunt Millie. 1943

agreed to absolve the Snowdens of the obligation to host our rambunctious crew on Christmas day, but it was a given they'd spend it with us, and they didn't argue.

Aunt Millie and Uncle 'D' were entirely devoted to one another and were inseparable. I hardly remember ever seeing one of them solo. Uncle 'D', a commercial artist, was a big man for his generation, over six feet tall with size thirteen feet that called for specialty shoes. Whenever I'd spot Aunt Millie trying on hats—her favorite accessory—in the Bay, I knew Uncle 'D' would be close at hand. Sure enough, I'd find the gentle giant just a table away, scanning the display with his artistic eye, his wife's purse comically swinging at his side. He was every bit as comfortable in that setting as she was poking through Ashdown's Hardware in support of his pursuits. Uncle 'D' loved cars, drove fast, and was the only person we knew who owned a car with a rumble seat.

Shopping with Aunt Millie and Ethel. 1939 Mountie dolls for Art and Frank.

Whenever he pulled up to our curb in that car, we were clamoring for a rumble ride before he had a chance to turn off the ignition.

Aunt Millie was an eccentric of sorts, absorbed in health food fads long before they came into vogue. We used to snicker at her fridge full of yogurt, wheat germ, and black strap molasses, the latter her cure for just about everything, including tooth aches. She was an advocate of six almonds a day, "palmed" her eyes religiously, and avoided doctors and dentists at all cost. We stopped snickering when she lived to the age of ninety-two, reading most print without the aid of eye glasses, and munching almonds with her own teeth.

We simply adored Aunt Millie and Uncle 'D', and knew they loved their nine nieces and nephews unreservedly. They were the life of the party at our Christmas gatherings and with a little coaxing, delivered the traditions we'd grown to expect from them. I best remember Uncle 'D' for two things—his unique rendition of *Jingle Bells*, which he loved, and the game of Tip-It, which he hated. But that didn't let him off the hook.

Tip-It consisted of two teams sitting across the dining room table from one another, one team in possession of a penny which members surreptitiously passed from hand to hand beneath the table.

"All hands on deck," our captain orders, and the tightly clenched fists of my team arise in unison, lining up in a row along the table. The opposing team must guess which hand holds the penny, either through elimination or by taking a bold, direct guess.

"Take that hand off," demands Don, pointing to my left hand, forcing me to open my fingers and reveal its contents. It's empty, so I remove it from the line-up, and the next opponent takes a guess. (If I'd held the penny, the round would have been over immediately—score one for the good guys.)

"Take that hand off," Audrey giggles, shyly tapping Uncle 'D's right hand. Again there's no penny, and another hand leaves the table. Then it's Art's turn to guess, and with no patience for this elimination stuff, he follows his instincts, and lunges at his mother's right hand, yelling "Tip-It!" If Aunt Mildred holds the penny in that hand, his team wins. All eyes are on Aunt Mildred as she tantalizes the opposition with a long hesitation, then slowly—ever so slowly—unfolds her fingers to reveal . . . she *has* the penny! Art's gamble pays off. The bad guys score, and we must part with the penny and become the guessers.

In defense of sounding like complete simpletons, we Kings had an ingenious knack for expanding the game beyond a moronic level, by implementing strategies to foil the opposition, such as feigning either guilt or innocence with a smirk or a roll of the eyes, or white-knuckling an empty hand while calmly relaxing the one holding the penny. Art, our resident clown, preferred the guessing side of the table where his theatrics could induce a penny holder to "tip his hand" or failing that, reduce Uncle 'D' to tears of laughter, cracking his resolve to hate this stupid game! I defy any family to create that much entertainment with a lowly penny.

King Family Improv

Uncle 'D' was a pioneer member of Calgary's chapter of "The Society for the Preservation and Encouragement of Barber Shop Quartet Singing in America" (SPEBSQSA), but once a year at Christmas he was compelled to perform solo—his unique Swedish version of *Jingle Bells*—for his eager nieces and nephews:

"Yingalala Bella
Yingalala Bella
Yingle all de vay
Oh vot fon eet ees to ride
In a von horse open sleigh-eh,
Oh vot fon eet ees to ride
In a von horse open sleigh..."

Aunt Millie, his biggest fan, then lead us into a chorus of laughter and applause that wouldn't stop until he obliged us with an encore. Usually, we demanded two.

The King's famous flare for dramatics was probably best personified by Uncle Walter, whose recitations—some his own compositions—vied with Charles Laughton's for my admiration. Our favorite was *Kissing Cup's Race*, a rousing 144 line poem by Campbell Rae Brown about a horse race, which Uncle Walter delivered at breakneck speed and nary a stumble. It didn't surprise me to learn that back in the twenties this recitation was the winning entry in an amateur talent contest at the Grand Theater. We adopted it as a Christmas tradition, and critical to the performance was a preamble of request and refusal. We'd ask, he'd refuse. We'd coax, he'd waver. We'd plead, and just when he had us on the brink of resignation, he'd gallop down the track leaving us in the starting gate:

> "You've never seen Kissing Cup, have you?
>   Stroll round to the paddock, my lord;
>   Just cast your eyes o'er the mare, sir,
>   You'll say that, upon your word,
>   You ne'er saw a grander shaped 'un
>   In all the whole course of your life.
>   Have you heard the strange story about her,
>   How she won Lord Hillboxton his wife?"

And who could forget the night, in the presence of Tina, a cherished friend of German descent, Uncle Walter recited an entire poem in her native tongue. There wasn't a dry eye in the house. Then there was the Christmas at our house that Dad—not to be outdone— brought us all to our knees by donning Mother's apron and our best antique lampshade to perform his uproarious rendition of *Take 'er To Jamaica Where The Rum Comes From*. It would have been impossible to convince an outsider that the performance was not rum assisted.

Summer Stock at '420'
Art, Stan, Ethel, Don, Frank, Marion. circa.1939

Two other games featured prominently in the King family collection: McGillicutty, a rowdy, senseless game of frivolity, mercifully restricted to the guys, and Charades, our signature favorite, unquestionably born from our theatrical heritage. Aunt Millie was always assigned the best charade slogans because the other female members of the clan were far too reserved to take on such meaty roles with any conviction. Her performance of Fourex Bakery's slogan, "The Freshest Thing in Town" brought the house down. She danced from one nephew's lap to the next, planting kisses—discreetly on the cheek, of course—leaving her team of guessers baffled, but falling off their chairs in laughter. Not to be denied her moment in the sun, she held the spotlight long after the clock ran out.

McGillicutty was usually undertaken by the biggest guys of the clan, Art, Frank and Ritchie. After clearing floor space, two brave volunteers wearing blindfolds would lie on the floor head to head with their left arms outstretched in a hand clasp, and their right hands gripping their weaponry—rolled up newspapers. Let the game begin! The striker yells, "Are you there McGillicutty?"— and McGillicutty's compulsory reply is met with a swift WHAP of the newspaper. McGillicutty might employ the defense maneuver of projecting his voice from one direction, then rolling his head to the opposite side to avoid the blow. The striker, however, might predict the strategy, and outsmart McGillicutty with a wicked offside WHAP. The striker and McGillicutty alternate roles after every strike, and on it goes.

The insanity of this game was, the striker was the only person who never knew when he'd landed a perfect head shot. We spectators screamed whether he hit or missed, and McGillicutty received all hits with stoic silence, unwilling to grant the striker any satisfaction by yelping OUCH! A winner, therefore, was never declared, so the game ended only when the intrepid warriors flailed themselves to exhaustion. I suppose it could be argued that the screaming onlookers were the winners, savoring all the hilarity, while suffering none of the abuse.

As the curtain fell on our incomparable Christmases, I often wondered about the uncle we never knew. The uncle stolen from us long before our time, by a war we didn't understand. Was our Uncle Arthur as funny as the others? Would he have invented stories as clever as Dad's? Did he ever recite *Kissing Cup's Race*? As fast as Uncle Walter? Might we have had more cousins? There was no end to the wondering.

Update:

Cousin Ethel and her husband John still live in the Elbow Park residence of her parents. Her goosnargh cakes are *almost* as good as her mother's. Cousin Art led *Kissing Cup* back to the track for us at a 2002 cousin reunion. Tears of nostalgia mingled with tears of laughter. Cousin Frank's family maintains the tradition of hit and run gift deliveries, raising the bar every year with their over-the-top stunts.

During a 1966 Christmas visit with Aunt Millie and Uncle 'D', to my eternal gratitude, my husband recorded Uncle 'D' singing his original version of *Jingle Bells* to our two oldest children, then ages five and three. We lost Uncle 'D' four years later, but he lives on in "Yingalala Bella." Aunt Millie's infectious laugh, captured on the same recording, is also alive and well. Their beautiful little retirement home on Britannia Drive was jacked up and carted from its choice lot to make way for a larger home.

King Cousin Reunion, 2002
Frank, Art, Rich, Don, Stan,
Ethel, Mar, Aud, Me

Chapter 13

–THE TEA KETTLE INN–

The King family purchased the Tea Kettle Inn in 1925, a restaurant operated by Mrs. Watson in the Blow Block just two doors from the King's residence, separated only by a beauty parlor. It was the second enterprise for my father's ambitious family, having already launched an antique business from their residence little more than a year prior. To everyone's sorrow, my grandfather enjoyed only a brief time with the antique business and did not live to see the inception of the restaurant. He died unexpectedly while in England on a buying trip in November, 1924. All the surviving members of the family shared equal voice in the decision-making of both concerns, but with Walter and

Tea Kettle Inn and House of Antiques. circa. 1931

Harry involved in teaching careers, Millie and Horace took over the reins of the restaurant, and their mother capably and enthusiastically ruled the antique shop. But for her, too, the joy was short-lived.

My grandmother died in June, 1928 and Harry, unwilling to let her dream die, resigned from his teaching position at Colonel Walker School, and without breaking stride, kept her beloved antique shop rolling. By 1931 the last of the siblings had married and vacated the family residence, and the restaurant relocated to the available space. The Tea Kettle Inn and the House of Antiques now stood side by side under one roof, their shared British influence melding in perfect harmony. For sixteen years the two businesses enjoyed many of the same patrons, and for me, stepping from one into the other through their adjoining door was as natural as padding from room to room in my own house.

In 1945, Walter, most recently engaged in war service duties in Redcliffe, moved his family to Calgary and took on a more active directorship in the businesses. A year later he launched a third enterprise, Property Sales, on adjacent property, including the family with directorships as custom dictated. For two brief years the four siblings worked elbow to elbow, their four signatures touchingly appearing one above the other on official documents preserved in my keeping today.

Then Uncle Harry's untimely death in 1947 brought about the first of the changes to come—the closing of The House of Antiques. Four years later, Uncle Walter, too, was gone, and his business sold to his working partner. Aunt Millie and Dad carried on gamely with the Tea Kettle Inn, but before long, Aunt Millie, fatigued and heavy hearted, made the decision to retire. Now it was one business and one brother.

My best memories of the Tea Kettle Inn begin with its inviting teapot in glowing red neon, hanging above its facade, irresistibly beckoning a wide range of customers to its doors: the office crowd, led by the Calgary Herald gang down the block, rushing back and forth for coffee breaks and lunch; the women shoppers, pouring in every afternoon to rest their weary feet with a "proper cup of tea"; the nightly capacity dinner crowd, generating a perennial assembly line of prime rib dinners and chicken pot pies; the country folk topping their Saturday ritual—a trip to the city for their week's supplies—with a bowl of Tea Kettle Inn mulligatawny soup; the frenetic summer tourist trade, that created a stampede of their own every Stampede week; and lastly, the theater crowd, demanding special menus and extended hours—a demand willingly accommodated by a tireless manager, since it offered him the opportunity to meet idols the likes of Sir John Martin Harvey and Vilma Banky.

A long, utilitarian, U-shaped counter with stools, shared the west half of the restaurant with the kitchen, and greeted everyone's arrival. The only adornment of note in this area was a set of four paintings I loved, depicting the fox hunt in England's lush countryside during the four seasons of the year—horses and hounds giving chase in spring, summer, fall and winter. The dining room filled the east side of the building with a small waiting lounge in the sunny front window and a huge, ornate antique buffet at the back. The east wall featured an ornamental fireplace with a profile of Queen Victoria, a braid of hair looping her ear, gracing one side, and her beloved consort, Prince Albert, facing her from the other.

Interior; Tea Kettle Inn. circa 1931

On the mantel sat a glass ship under a dome, backed by a large mirror reflecting the intricate details of its port side. The story goes that the ship had arrived from England badly damaged, and Dad, using his skilled watchmaker's fingers, painstakingly glued every miniscule ladder, rope, mast and sailor back into place. I was utterly captivated by that ship, and remember pressing my nose up against the dome to examine all its teeny tiny parts. Dad's miraculous repair job was beautifully perfect—and perfectly beautiful! Further along that same wall hung a gigantic oil painting of a shoemaker with a young lad at his feet, absorbed in the handiwork of the master—almost as absorbed as I was in the ship.

The burden of the restaurant's day to day operation must have constantly weighed on Dad, but the responsibility of it rarely entered my carefree mind. For me it was a place where I could breeze through the doors and be assured of the same warm, motherly greeting I got at home. And there was always a pot of heavenly homemade soup on the stove, which I didn't get at home. I was a "Campbell's kid" in the Scarboro kitchen.

Dad entered the business as a young bachelor of twenty-three without an ounce of experience in the food industry, but a huge desire to learn and succeed, and enough energy to coast through sixteen-hour days, six days a week. He was a devout Christian, however, and refused to open the business on the day of rest, a day he set aside for church and family, desiring his staff to do likewise. But he sometimes attended to office matters on Sunday after church, and I frequently tagged along for some precious solitary time with him.

The moment Dad disappeared to his basement office, I'd hit the soda fountain, launching my attack with a modest scoop of ice cream and a vow of discipline. But those darn toppings got to me every time. I'd squish, squish, squish my way right down the row of flavors, my ice cream vanishing under a volcano of chocolate, butterscotch, maple walnut, strawberry and caramel. Then I'd lick the spoon and the dish, and still not satisfied, ask Dad if we could take a pie home for dinner. It was my good fortune that Dad also had a sweet tooth, and always agreed. Sundays were good. At least until one calamitous Sunday.

"Dad, can Helen and Jean come with us today? They've never had a ride in our delivery truck."

"Of course they can come. Hop in quick, I'm ready to go."

The three of us scamper through the back door of the Tea Kettle Inn panel truck, and park ourselves on the floor of the cargo area, where we giggle and carry on all the way downtown. While Dad tends to business, I take my friends on a guided tour of all the yummy parts of the restaurant. Unknown to us, during the course of the afternoon, Dad slips the family's customary Sunday pie into the back of the truck, in the space meant for pies—not kids.

"Time!" he calls out, "All aboard for home."

We race for the truck and fling open the doors. Only as Helen raises her foot to clamber inside, does Dad tumble to imminent disaster.

"Watch out for the pi_" he warns . . . too late. I gasp at the sight of Helen's foot planted—firmly and squarely—in the middle of a cherry pie. We had canned peaches for dessert that Sunday.

Where There's a Will

In the beginning, the Tea Kettle Inn struggled to establish a clientele as any new business does, then just as it was daring to believe, the dark cloud of the Great Depression rolled in, and hung menacingly overhead. With the restaurant's survival threatened daily, Dad resolved to address each crisis as it arose, hour by hour and penny by penny, employing his resourceful ingenuity to every detailed aspect of the business. He even trekked through the snow one blustery Sunday afternoon to the Mount Royal residence of his banker, rapped on the door and pleaded for a loan extension. He got it. His arrival on foot, evidence of having sacrificed his car to the cause, no doubt went a long way to clinch the deal.

Aunt Millie and Joan, her kitchen *protégé*, came up with the creative idea of developing specially priced menus each day, and distributing them to surrounding offices in an attempt to lure customers. One by one, the dining room staff became caught up in the battle for survival, voluntarily joining the delivery corps to spread the word, and rejoicing with their boss as new customers trickled in. I'm sure this early personal involvement of employees helped cement the loyalty they displayed for the life of the business. Joan continued to serve the company for as long as I can remember.

Another brain wave which became a wildly successful drawing card, was a teacup reader, Mother Shipton, whose name they plucked from the history books—a sixteenth century seer who had apparently predicted the destruction of the Spanish Armada and the Great Fire of London. Our twentieth century Mother Shipton, however, made no predictions on that grand a scale, but amazed the customers never-the-less with morsels of accurate information, not gleaned from floating tea leaves, but from notes slipped to her on the sly by management. I don't know if Mother Shipton foresaw her own demise, but when Dad observed the alarming extent to which his customers were falling under her spell, his conscience dictated shipping her out.

The restaurant became a fully self sufficient operation with its every facet taking place on the premises. It did its own butchering, baking and laundry, using soap made from carefully saved cooking fat. Leftover vegetables and meat determined the next day's *soup de jour,* and extra fruit, either fresh or from day old pies, was transformed into its trademark dessert, steamed fruit pudding, my all time favorite. Most everyone who lived through the depression developed a frugal lifestyle which they maintained forever after, and the restaurant was no exception. Dad never sought ways to skim the customer, but was consciously committed to a no-waste policy through good times and bad.

Dad's "Girls"

Dad had an instinctive talent for hiring girls of exemplary character and natural abilities, and made certain they were adequately trained and at ease before putting them on the floor. He respected each girl, and opened his heart and his home to them, a courtesy they returned with a devotion uncommon in the restaurant industry. In turn, he took the unprecedented step of offering company shares to some of his long term devotees.

We adored Dad's girls and became intimately acquainted with many of them, from hostesses and waitresses, to cooks and

Dad and his Girls. 1935

dishwashers. Teresa, in fact, began as a laundress, and later moved in with our family to become a much cherished nanny—the very nanny who warmed my crib bedding with her iron in readiness for my first arrival. Lucky me. Ann and Marie held special places in Dad's heart when he was invited to give them away at their weddings. It broke his heart, when a few short years after Marie's wedding, he carried out the grievous duty of informing her that her dashing young groom had been killed in the war. Ann had two sisters who worked in the restaurant at various times, a situation repeated with a number of sisters. Tina, a dedicated supervisor, lived in our home for a few years during my teens, sharing my room and filling the role of the adored big sister I longed for. She was indispensable to Mother, in the ever increasing clutches of her ghastly mood disorder.

Edna, Margaret, Tina, Julie, Eleanor. circa. 1948

Phyllis, an early secretary, was a frequent guest in our home, and we've never witnessed a finer example of dedication to duty than the time she stayed with Don and me while Mother and Dad traveled. It seems they made off with the only tube of toothpaste, and Phyl, determined we must not miss even one crucial brushing, demonstrated the use of Lux bar soap as a substitute.

As foam cascaded down her chin and our faces registered appropriate horror, she cheerfully, though unconvincingly, mumbled, "Mm, Mm, Good!" We didn't buy in. Years prior to secretarial (and dental) duties, our resourceful Phyl bounced through a multitude of positions from lowly pantry girl to the frightening responsibility of charge duties in Aunt Millie's absence. She handled them all like a pro. It was a sad day for our family when we lost Phyl to Ottawa, where she took up a position as a private legal secretary.

Annie came to the Tea Kettle as a young farm girl, quaking at the very thought of her first job waitressing, but with coaching and encouragement, she soared to the top as a self-assured supervisor in whose hands Dad could confidently trust every particular of the business. One of Annie's daily duties was to print the menus, which she performed to her renowned perfection on our ancient, unforgiving Gestetner. I used to watch in wonder as she rolled absolutely spotless menus out of that grimy, archaic contraption.

I can still see Ruth, with her upswept hair, flying through the dining room, serving her customers with such speed and efficiency they'd pass up empty tables to wait for an available one in her station. She collected a mint in tips. Then there was Rose, whose station usually included our favorite corner table, and who needed no reminding of our personal desires—extra gravy on Stan's mashed potatoes, a second dessert for Dad, and steamed fruit pudding for me, if it was on the menu. She was even more disappointed than I when it wasn't. Dad used to aptly remark that our soft, gracious Rose, "sure knows how to put down a plate." And who could forget the infectious laugh of Louise, the jovial cook who made the best soup on the planet; the indomitable spirit of Mrs. Saul, who for twenty-six years turned the drudgery of dishwashing into a cheerful work of art, an achievement that was

201

rewarded with a special pension throughout her retirement; or the pride of Arthur Beckson, who faithfully scrubbed and scoured the building within an inch of its life for twenty years. I don't think he ever missed a day.

"Becksy" was a diminutive, weather-beaten bachelor, who had an old tweed cap permanently glued to his head, the perfect complement for his toothless grin. He appeared to be utterly alone in the world, never breathing a word of any family, so we embraced him as ours. We first encountered Becksy at the residence when he turned up looking for work, and Mother supplied him with a bucket, some rags and a bar of Bon Ami, and pointed him in the direction of the storm windows. When Dad came home to the sparkling result, he hired Becksy on the spot, and that was the beginning of a beautiful friendship.

After Becksy retired, he paid us a daily visit to the restaurant. He'd come in the alley door and down the back stairs to the basement office where Elsie, Dad's bookkeeper, always greeted him with the same question.

"Hello Becksy, are you hungry?"

"Oh no, Mrs. Duncan," he replies, looking at his feet and shaking his head, "I'm not hungry."

"But you'll have a bit of lunch, won't you Becksy?"

"Oh no, Mrs. Duncan, I just ate."

Then Elsie dispenses with any further patter, stretches her four feet eleven inches all the way to five feet, and marches upstairs to the kitchen, returning shortly with a steaming plate of roast beef and Yorkshire pudding. Mashed potatoes and gravy, too. Becksy—still shaking his head and denying hunger—ties into it like he hasn't eaten for a week. Then Elsie slips some change into his pocket and he's on his way.

The routine never varied—unless Becksy turned up on a winter day without an overcoat.

"Becksy, where's your coat?"

"I'm not sure, Mrs. Duncan."

"Was it stolen again, Becksy?"—a reasonable question considering the seedy, east-end apartment he rents—shocking living quarters Dad regularly tries to budge him from, without success.

"Well, maybe," he replies, hanging his head lower than ever in embarrassment.

"Becksy, sit down and don't move until I come back," Elsie orders in her bossiest lieutenant commander voice, throwing on her coat and boots and scooping a handful of bills from the petty cash box. She scurries down to the Salvation Army Thrift Shop and returns fifteen minutes later with a coat, which she buttons him into like a little boy she's readying for kindergarten. He turns to leave, and one final order follows him down the hall.

"Now Becksy, don't lose this one. I can't keep buying coats, you know, and you'll catch your death without one."

Becksy was well loved by his adoptive family, and on his death, his next of kin—my father—arranged a small funeral service for him, and secured a burial plot. Arthur Beckson deserved a proper send-off.

The Inspector General

A 1930's Tea Kettle Inn letterhead reads, "All cooking under the personal supervision of Mrs. Mildred Snowden." It didn't lie. Not a plate left *her* kitchen without her scrutiny, and approval was granted only when it met the rigid standards she applied to entertaining at home: piping hot plates, piping hot food, not too much food for the size of the plate, no sauce or gravy dribbling off the edge, and no cracks or chips in the china. Her eagle eyes— front and back—constantly scanned ovens, grills and pots, and her system of perpetually rotating foods effectively eliminated the limp, dried-out products of warming trays. As a testament to the trusted cooking skills of his sister and her female staff, Dad's advertising features always boasted "Women Cooks."

Aunt Millie's daily menu selections were created from personally tested recipes, and prices were competitive. A 1949 Stampede Souvenir Menu offered a breakfast of "'Chuckhouse' Ham & Eggs with Toast" for 65 cents, and seven cents got you a good cup of coffee. But not a refill. Dinner included "Alberta Red Label T-Bone Steak" with all the trimmings for $1.65 or "Grilled Pork Tenderloin" for $1.10. Top of the line was a "Choice 'Pride of the Prairies' Buffalo Steak" for $2.00. Dad maintained a personally typed loose leaf book of recipes, each with his initialed approval. Whenever I flip through it today, I see him smacking his lips as he scratched 'HK' at the bottom of every page. I'd wager he taste tested the dessert recipes more than once.

Our in-house inspector general also lined up her staff for inspection military style before they went on duty. Hair, nails, uniforms, hose and shoes had to pass the test before anyone stepped into the kitchen or onto the floor. I doubt if anyone reported for duty unprepared more than once. Some of the girls developed rituals above and beyond the call.

Ruth, Dorothy, Kay. 1948

I remember Ruth using a stool rather than a chair in the staff room for her lunch breaks, so she could slide her stiffly starched apron 180 degrees around her waist, and let it hang off the back of the stool to prevent lap crease. She wouldn't think of removing it entirely, condemning herself to the impossible task of replicating all the folds and creases of the original bow.

Aunt Millie and Dad set the standard with their own impeccable grooming. Dad stepped out the door every morning in a pressed suit—gray or navy—with suspendered pants, a crisply starched French cuffed shirt—always white—and garters above and below; an upper arm slinky-style pair to restrain his shirt sleeves, and an elasticized set on his calves to prevent his hose from slumping. His first mission arriving home from work every night—every single night—was to polish his shoes, a duty he performed while still wearing them. I'd be bursting with news of my day's events, so I'd follow him to the basement, and he'd listen attentively to my full account above the snapping of the cloth. I also remember a brief period when he began showing up mid day with his decorum comically shaken. He'd installed new milk dispensers to replace the single serving bottles, and couldn't seem to get the hang of hoisting the replacement canister into place without dumping the first serving all over his suit. He came within one dry cleaning bill of returning to the pesky half-pint bottles.

After Aunt Millie's retirement, Dad developed an employees' handbook in an effort to maintain her standards. It included "House Policy" and "General Information," but focused largely on "Personal Cleanliness," stressing cleanliness from the inside out—the inside including the mind as well as the underwear! In no uncertain terms, he expressed his daily demands for: bathing; the use of deodorant; clean underwear, uniforms and hose (with seams straight); hair nets over "non elaborate" hairdo's; no "unnatural" make-up, nail polish or jewelry, except wedding bands ("bad taste when in uniform") and hand washing after every eventuality, from a visit to the washroom to merely touching the face or hair. Money was considered a serious contaminant, so food handlers *never* doubled as cashiers. Serving trays were also considered germ breeders and never used.

An additional detailed book of "Pointers For Waitresses" included: "be friendly, but not talkative; know your city to be helpful to tourists; don't gossip; tell your boyfriends it's not that we don't appreciate their business, but ...; help customers with coats (lone women only, except in the case of elderly men, or young men if they have a physical handicap); don't be a tip chaser, give good service because it's the right thing to do." Waitresses recorded all orders in their heads, Dad insisting that eye contact goes further to aid the memory than a pencil. The end result was a string of crackerjack waitresses who could balance piping hot plates for a table of six up their towel-padded arms and present each one to the right party, with all special requests observed: Mr. Smith's roast beef well done, with peas instead of carrots, and

Mrs. Smith's beef rare without gravy. The Tea Kettle amassed a large clientele that was as loyal as its staff.

The Engines That Could

Dad and his sister were the original engines that could—no mountain was too steep to climb. They chugged through every predicament with indomitable determination. My favorite story of Dad took place during Stampede week one summer when I was hostessing for him. The place was hopping and every high chair we owned was pressed into service. I was able to provide a table for a young family, but not a high chair for their toddler. Dad spotted the dilemma, flew out the door and dashed across the street to the Hudson's Bay, returning scant minutes later bearing the required item. He was still tearing the price tag off as he swept it to the party's table. I couldn't imagine how he'd achieved a purchase transaction in that short a time. Well, he hadn't. He'd simply made a beeline for the infant's furniture department, plucked out the first sturdy looking chair that caught his eye, marched it onto the escalator and out the door. At the first opportunity, he phoned the Bay, and confessed his shoplifting gambit to the dumbfounded manager, requesting the charge be added to his account.

Dad employed another bold strategy during the busy lunch hour with remarkable diplomacy and success. If he had a single customer waiting for a table, he'd approach a seated single with an appeal to share their table, offering a guilt-free option to refuse. He knew his customers well, and had a knack for recommending compatible pairings (always the same sex—heaven forbid), and it was intriguing what an enjoyable lunch resulted for parties who accepted the invitation. My recommendations for romantic pairings never got to first base.

That same summer Dad taught me the fundamental lesson for a successful business, and I never forgot it. I was appalled at his response to a disgruntled customer; not only refusing payment, but encouraging a return visit "on the house." "We'll starve to death if you keep giving away free meals," was my impulsive reaction, a statement I can only defend with a plea of temporary insanity. This business was clearly feeding our family well—without my genius—and to Dad's credit, he charitably refrained from reminding me of the fact. But he did hammer home the point that a business is not built on a customer coming through your doors once, but on him coming back. With that, I gently informed him of the vacationing American who'd erupted when confronted with the unthinkable truth that his dollar was worth ninety-eight cents in Canada that day. I had a feeling he would not be back.

Aunt Millie made it a regular habit to emerge from the kitchen and mingle with the customers for feedback. When spotting a new patron early one morning, she approached.

"Good morning, sir, welcome to the Tea Kettle Inn. Is everything satisfactory with your breakfast?"

"My breakfast is just fine ma'am, except I have to say, your bacon isn't as good as the bacon served at the York Hotel."

Aunt Millie, noticeably distressed with the gentleman's reply, marches directly to her pint-sized office squeezed into the back of the kitchen, and dials the manager of the York Hotel Coffee Shop.

"This is the Tea Kettle Inn calling. Would you mind sharing some information with me? I'd like to know where you get your bacon."

"I'm terribly sorry, Mrs. Snowden, but we don't divulge that kind of information."

Never one to lower her dignity, Aunt Millie resists the temptation to slam down the phone. Instead she calmly places the receiver in its cradle and hatches a plan. At the crack of dawn the next morning, she prowls the alley behind the York Hotel until she locates their delivery entrance. Then she waits . . . and waits . . . and waits. When the Burn's Meat truck finally rolls in, you can't wipe the triumphant grin off her face as she dances all the way back to the Tea Kettle and picks up the phone.

"Hello, Burns? Mildred Snowden of the Tea Kettle Inn. I'd like to place a bacon order please."

She wasn't averse to dashing to the nearest bakery for a coconut cream pie either, if a customer expressed a heart's desire, and our own bakery couldn't provide. She did whatever it took to satisfy a customer.

Uninvited Guests

The Tea Kettle had a number of back door guests. In fact, a ritual of activity took place daily among the hungry scrounging for their daily food supply through the garbage bins in the alley behind. Two men in particular, I remember well. One pulled a flatbed cart with two enormous wooden wheels up and down the alley, loading it with food scraps and any other kind of scrap that caught his fancy. I had no idea where he parked his cart or himself at night, but I knew I could count on him returning on schedule the next day. The other man used to sit on the back stoop in the summer, and drain all the fly-infested single-serving milk bottles awaiting pickup, until he'd squeezed out a small serving for himself. It was a troubling situation Dad never knew quite how to handle, so he left the men to their own devices.

A whole different sort of activity took place in the evenings, directly across the alley at the Empress Hotel. Its segregated entrances intrigued me, with their overhead neon signs specifying one door for "Men" and another for "Ladies and Escorts." The elegant tone implied by the very terms *Ladies and Escorts* seemed incongruous to me with a back alley bar entrance, especially when an overwhelming number of female patrons did not meet my definition of ladies. I remember the night a disoriented empress from the Empress stumbled through the restaurant's back door, creating quite a disturbance in the kitchen. She was no lady.

Other guests were far more troublesome, like the one who broke into Dad's basement office on a Sunday, blasted the safe to smithereens with nitroglycerin, and scooped up the two-day take from the restaurant and the antique shop, leaving the place in a shambles. That was one Monday morning Dad's usual high spirits were dampened. The culprit was eventually captured and convicted, and Dad, following one of his favorite credos that "every soul is a royal soul," visited his transgressor in prison to extend a hand of forgiveness and a plea to reform. He received no encouragement, and I believe that was the end of it.

One other time, on a day I'd joined Dad for my Sunday sundae, we found the back door smashed open, and assumed an intruder had come and gone. Bracing for the worst, we headed directly for the safe, but it was intact. The cash register? It was undisturbed, also. We moved stealthily through the entire premises, and not until we entered the bakery, located in the far corner of the basement, was the mystery solved. Sprawled on the floor beneath one of the work tables was the scruffiest looking derelict I'd ever seen, blissfully unconscious with a giant bottle of vanilla—empty—firmly gripped in one hand. Dad was annoyed to say the least and summoned the police to cart him away. I was grateful the scruffy reprobate had gone for the vanilla and not my Sunday take-home pie.

The real talk of the town was a Saturday night hold-up just before closing, in which the trembling cashier followed her instructions to the letter, emptying the till and handing over every penny without resistance. But the armed robber got the surprise of his life when one loyal waitress appeared on the scene just as he was scooping up the last of the loot. Unable to bear the thought of someone running off with her revered boss's money, she vaulted the counter and gave chase, up and down streets and alleys for blocks, before, to her everlasting regret, exhaustion overtook her. But I doubt the chase was in vain—I gave it better odds for affecting a cure to the sinful ways of a crook than Dad's jail house visit did.

I thought a lot about that armed robber the next time I made my two-block morning trek to the Bank of Nova Scotia on Eighth Avenue (now Rococo Restaurant) to deposit the prior day's take. It was my habit to nonchalantly walk the same route, the same time, carrying the same bag of money, every day, with never a fear of ambush. Overnight I began altering my routine, and just as abruptly, Dad began sending me off with a firm directive to "hand over the bag" without any heroics.

Just Desserts

The main course was never enough for Dad. From the beginning he viewed the restaurant as a venue for serving food for the soul as well as the body. In the thirties, he launched the "Tea Kettle Inn Kritics Klub," a group of business men who met regularly in the basement to debate issues of the day. Meetings often followed an actual debate format with two members taking up opposing arguments of a selected topic. Dad thrived on taking the unpopular side, and especially loved the challenge of going head to head against Val Milvain, a young lawyer whose occupation he secretly envied. It came as no surprise to him when, some forty years later, his friendly adversary became Chief Justice of Alberta.

Dad also combined his interest in the law with his love of

theater by writing courtroom dramas, in which he designed roles for his circle of friends. He was always the flamboyant lawyer for the defense, of course. As I understand it, the members of his rep company were content to imagine their potential for greatness, rather than risk the verdict of an audience, but it didn't stop them from constructing a temporary stage in an unused upstairs office in the neighboring Blow Block. From it, the wanna-be's went on to greater heights.

The makeshift theater was also adopted for staff Christmas parties, and Dad wrote some inspirational plays in which consenting employees were cast in roles such as Humility, Forgiveness, or Charity. But Uncle Walter pulled out all stops for his play based on the life of Louis XIV, casting Brother Don in the lead as the innocent child King, and Cousin Art as Cardinal Mazarin, the power behind the throne. The staff gave them a standing ovation (did they have a choice?) and Don's Thespian aspirations were once again gratified, at least for the moment. He was less enthused the year Uncle Walter gave him star billing as Santa, gluing on a beard so firmly that it was days of pain and suffering before it was entirely removed. "Why didn't he assign the role to Uncle 'D'?" Don complained. "He's the perfect size for Santa, and he can grow his own beard."

Dad also had a propensity for seeking out needy individuals about town and gathering them under his wing. I especially remember delivering food, clothing and toys to a destitute family with four children, eking out a subsistence in the cramped quarters above their father's dilapidated East End Mission. They were only marginally better off than the forsaken flock they served. I was extremely uncomfortable visiting that sad family, and Mother especially sympathized with the woman of the house. Don never forgot the day he was given a desirous set of toy houses by neighbors who were moving away, and Dad immediately whisked them off to his charity family. We were all unhappy when we learned, years later, that our missionary fled the city with parish funds, and eventually duped his own children out of bonds donated by my father, earmarked for their education.

But for intrigue, nothing could top the the annual house call Dad made to the home of the mysterious, reclusive Miss Moss, a character plucked from the pages of a Dickens novel. Miss Moss lived like Miss Havisham behind heavy, dust-laden curtains in a decaying, two-story house opposite Central Park (now Memorial Park), never stepping foot into the outside world. She retained a neighbor boy by phone to fetch supplies, creaking open the back door just wide enough to receive them and slip him the cash payment. We used to imagine the phantom delivery boy's name must be "Pip."

I never knew how or when the practice began, but Dad called on Miss Moss every Christmas Eve to deliver a turkey dinner with all the trimmings. She not only received him—and his tray—at the *front* door, but actually allowed him inside, a privilege we doubt she granted anyone else. On Boxing Day, she'd skid the empty tray out onto the front porch for pickup, so he was never granted a second entry. For years Don and I begged Dad to let us accompany him on his intriguing "Moss Mission," but he refused in deference to her sensitivities. Finally the day came when he relented, trusting we'd attained an acceptable degree of maturity and decorum.

"Do you think she'll let us inside?" I ask Don, as we huddle in the back seat of the car on the drive over, out of our minds with excitement.

"Now, you two," Dad cautions over his shoulder, "I've warned you that she probably won't invite you in, so be prepared to accept her choice graciously." Dad continues to caution and warn throughout the entire drive.

My heart is booming in my chest as we climb her groaning front steps, Dad balancing the festive Tea Kettle Inn tray on his shoulder, Don and I seeking refuge behind. Our knock is swiftly met with a curtain sliding back, just far enough to reveal a ghostly eyeball examining each of us in slow motion. Then the curtain relaxes, and we can hear shuffling footsteps approach the door. After an interminable wait, a seemingly detached hand inches it open, and the same ghostly eyeball peers through the crack. Then a head pokes around the door.

"Good evening, Mr. King. How kind of you to come."

"Good evening, Miss Moss. I'd like you to meet my children, Donald and Eleanor."

"Hello children. It's lovely to meet you. Your father is always so good to me."

There's an anguishing moment of indecision when the four of us seem frozen in our tracks, and I'm murmuring to myself, *"Please, p-l-e-a-s-e invite us in,"* my imagination running wild over what's inside.

Suddenly, Miss Moss opens the door fully, and waves us through. I'm beside myself. All Dad's courtesy instructions are flying out the window as my eyes dart about indiscreetly, attempting to absorb the unbelievable spectacle before me—a lifetime of newspapers, periodicals and nondescript collectibles stockpiled from floor to ceiling. I can barely discern the outline of a piano in its burial site in the corner of the living room. I quickly determine that the Tea Kettle Inn tray must hold the distinction of being the only item to ever enter *and exit* this house.

Then Dad breaks the tension, "Do you get outside for some fresh air, Miss Moss? It's so good for you, you know." Don and I are turning ourselves inside out over Dad's audacity asking such a question, when he knows full well the answer.

Miss Moss's surprising reply is more outrageous than the

question. Leaning in close, she whispers an assurance, "Oh yes, Mr. King, I took a walk in the park one balmy evening last July— veiled, of course!"

On that note, we wished her compliments of the season and went our way, mission accomplished. My unforgettable day between the covers of *Great Expectations!*

In the forties, Dad launched two other establishments, catering mostly to the working crowd on coffee or lunch breaks— the T-Kettle Kounter located at 231 - 8th Avenue West, a small, but high volume operation that ran from 1941-1949, and a second T-Kettle Kounter at 1110 - 6th Street West, operating for only two years during 1946 and 1947. I remember little of either, probably because my sentiments were so firmly attached to the "Inn," his first and most successful enterprise. Then in 1950, Dad formed a new partnership with Reuben Mottishaw and his son Roy. The Mottishaws arrived with considerable experience in the industry, most recently managing the York Hotel Coffee Shop (where they served Burns bacon). The newly formed Company pooled ideas for a new restaurant, and in July of that year, The Carolina opened in the Jubilee Block at 619 Centre Street under Roy's management.

Although the Tea Kettle Inn and the Carolina shared product and service ideas, and exchanged staff when necessary, each had a distinctly different clientele, and however much I grew to love the Carolina, I still remained unabashedly partial to my first love, the Tea Kettle Inn. I suspect the same was true for long standing regulars like the friendly, animated senior couple who always sat in the center of the dining room, she wearing a garish, lopsided wig and jumbo rouge balls on her cheeks, one higher than the other as if she applied everything standing on an inclined plane; or the middle-aged unsighted man, more comfortable by the wall, where he listened attentively as his waitress read him the day's menu, his faithful guide dog stationed quietly at his feet; or the elegant young couple who sought the table by the fireplace, beneath my glass ship, with their perfectly behaved Shirley Temple child perched angelically in a high chair between them; or the King family, observing them all from their Saturday night table in the back corner, over tea and steamed fruit pudding.

During the war, the government appealed to the restaurant community to form an organization to address war related problems in the industry, which resulted in the establishment of the Canadian Restaurant Association. Dad served as National President in 1948, a year he spent exchanging ideas with fellow restaurateurs across the country, encouraging participation everywhere from small towns to major cities. From Halifax to Victoria, he gave speeches on issues such as cost control, sanitation standards and the importance of serving wholesome meals. His greatest desire was for the industry to accept a leadership role in the health of the nation.

It was an exhilarating year of travel for Dad, and a year of adventure for me, with exciting trips to the airport, where I could stand on the tarmac to wave hello or good-bye as his plane taxied past. On a couple of occasions I was even allowed to board briefly and sit in his seat. And of course, I eagerly helped him unpack when he returned from a trip, just in case there was something for me in the bottom of his suitcase. I was never disappointed.

On September 22, 1947, my tenth birthday, Dad was attending an Association conference in Toronto—an indoctrination into his forthcoming role as president. He was swamped with speeches and presentations the entire day—but not too swamped to forget a promise to his daughter—to tell her the true story of her arrival.

And so, at the end of a long, exhausting day, he sat down in his hotel room, uncapped his fountain pen, and on Royal York Hotel stationery, began...

"*My dear little El,*

I did not find you in a basket.

You were ours from the very beginning..."

– AFTERWORD –

In 1956, I entered the Calgary General Hospital School of Nursing, its gleaming new residence becoming my home for the next three years. In these first eighteen years of my life, Calgary's population had more than doubled, from 85,000 to 180,000. Little did I know that day I moved across town, how much further my world was about to be altered. With Stan now residing in the United States and Don attending the University of British Columbia, the Scarboro nest had emptied. It broke my heart to see Mother and Dad's world begin to crumble.

Mother's depressions increased in frequency and severity, and specialists consulted far and wide could only offer temporary relief, at best. Meanwhile, Dad was engaged in his own health battle, suffering severe anxiety, ultimately determined to be the precursor to Parkinson's Disease which followed in its wake. He was an early recipient of cryosurgery which successfully relieved his tremor, but failed to halt the progressive rigidity causing gait and speech impairment. Under these overwhelming circumstances, he made two gut-wrenching decisions—to part with the business and soon after, the house.

The Tea Kettle Inn closed its doors in the spring of 1958, having lived to witness Calgary's first parkade and adjoining plus 15 rise above its roofline. To my eternal gratitude, its elegant facade was spared the indignity of obliteration by an LRT station, the kiss of death for many businesses on the block. Slowly, the street slid into decay. I understand my beloved glass ship met a terrible fate—confetti in a dustpan. Other memorabilia slipped into oblivion—the neon sign, the buffet, the shoemaker, Victoria and Albert. I hope they're loved, wherever they are. The company was sold to Dad's partner, Roy Mottishaw, and the building itself to National Bakery, which operated from that location until the mid nineties. The Carolina absorbed staff devotees who wished to remain with the business, eventually closing its doors in 1976, when Roy moved on to new ventures.

By 1961 the stairs in the Scarboro home had become too difficult for Dad to negotiate, so we all bid it a tearful farewell, and Mother and Dad settled into a bungalow in Scarboro Heights—on the other side of the coulee.

Dad died in October, 1984 at the age of eighty-two. Seven of his Tea Kettle "girls" attended his funeral, twenty-six years after the restaurant's closure. Mother died less than a year later in September, 1985, also age eighty-two, and the girls lovingly returned to honor her. I was thrilled to learn, since the death of my parents, that twenty-six former employees gathered from near and far in 1990 to reminisce their good times at the "Inn."

The Calgary General Hospital—renamed Bow Valley Centre—along with our beloved nurse's residence, vanished in a cloud of dust on October 4, 1998. My first home away from home—blasted into history at the tender age of forty-two.

—ACKNOWLEDGEMENTS—

My grateful thanks to the following for
helping me build my house:

My brothers, cousins, school mates and friends who
contributed invaluable stories and photos, assisted my shaky memory
and backed me throughout with their interest and encouragement—not
to mention a preliminary reading that pushed me to nail down the roof.

Catharine Warren—a friend from Scarboro days—
who gave generously of her time to dig into the corners of the basement
and sweep away the clutter.

Gayl Veinotte, editor extraordinaire, whose creative decorating ideas
motivated my house to stop talking and start singing.

Sherry Ward, wonder woman graphic designer, whose imagination and
genius dressed it up, set it on its toes and sent it dancing.

An honorable mention to Aunt Lil—the last of our family's senior
generation—my faithful consultant and correspondent, who died
at age ninety-four during the writing of this book, having dutifully
answered the last of my questions.

And without saying, my love and gratitude for my husband, Dick,
my nominee for sainthood for patiently enduring—without complaint—
forty-three years of the "King Family Players" repeated,
ridiculous performances. And they continue...

—PHOTO ACKNOWLEDGMENTS—

All photos and memorabilia from the King family collection
with the exception of:

On the Roof (pgs. 60, 61) — Helen Hamilton

Home from School (p. 94) — Helen Hamilton

Grade Nine Party (p. 100) — Helen Hamilton

In Our Hudson Bays (p. 117) — Lois Wilkins

CGIT Camp (p. 122) — Mary Nelson

Ritchie, Rags, Bobby (p. 127) — John MacLeod

Jean on Strawberry (p. 129) — Helen Hamilton

Pyjama Party (p. 152) — Helen Hamilton

Mary & Mike (p. 154) — Mary Nelson

Skyline Menu (p. 156) — Carolyn Kelly

Mask Designers (p. 173) — Helen Hamilton

Halloween Dummy (p. 174) — Helen Hamilton

Tea Kettle Inn and House of Antiques (p. 191) — Glenbow Archives

Tea Kettle Inn Waitresses (pgs. 199, 204) — Kay Wilson

House backscreenings from painting by Joan Fedoroshyn

Memorabilia photographed by Sherry Ward

—BIBLIOGRAPHY—

Accounts by Calgary Authors, *Young People of All Ages, Sports,*
   Schools and Youth Groups. Century publications, 1975.

Articles from the Calgary Herald spanning 1995-2003.
   In particular, columnists:
   Bly, David—*Heritage;* Bobrovitz, Jennifer—*Cornerstones*;
   Brennan, Brian—*Tribute;* Parker, David—*About Town.*

Centennial Book Committee, Central United Church, Calgary.
   They Gathered at the River, A Centennial History.
   Central United Church, 1975.

Connery, Allan, compiler. *As Reported in The Herald.*
   The Calgary Herald, 1982.

Foran, Max. *Calgary—An Illustrated History. Photos assembled*
   by Edward Cavell. James Lorimer & Company Publishers—and—
   National Museum of Man, National Museums of Canada,
   Toronto, 1978.

McNeill, Leishman. *Tales of the Old Town.* The Calgary Herald, 1950.

Peach, Jack. *All Our Yesteryears.* The Calgary Herald, 1986.

Peach, Jack. *The First Hundred Years.* The Calgary Chamber of
   Commerce, 1990.

Shiels, Bob. *Calgary, A not too solemn look at Calgary's first 100 years.*
   The Calgary Herald, 1975.

Sparks, Susie, editor. *Calgary, A Living Heritage.*
   The Junior League of Calgary, 1984.